From the Editor

I've known from the first time I saw Kara Henry's layouts that she has a gift for getting straight to the heart of the story with meaningful journaling. Photos tell a lot in scrapbooking, but the story becomes much more complete when you add words. Yet it is often a daunting task to find the words to express all you'd like to say, and many of us give up before the story is complete.

Because journaling is so central to scrapbooking, we wanted to bring you a book filled with suggestions, prompts and tips to help you more fully record your memories. With her own deep conviction about the importance of the written word in scrapbooks, Kara was up for the challenge. She has created a book chock full of ideas to get you past writer's block and on to meaningful journaling.

To quote Kara: "My own writing has evolved since I started scrapbooking, and along the way, I've realized that words have a force all their own. They have the power to encourage, to heal, to make us laugh and to express love—things we could all use a little more of!"

We could not agree more! So don't let your story go untold—let Kara help you get it straight from your heart into your scrapbooks.

Publisher Chad Harvie

Editor in Chief Pam Baird

Assistant Editor Tammy Morrill

Contributing Editor/Designer Jeri Hulsh

Editorial Staff
Alisha Gordon, Kara Henry, Jana Johnson, Paige Taylor

Art Director Amy Noorda

Design
Linda Nelson, Hannah Craner

Cover Photography Kaycee Leishman

Photography
Linda Nelson, Mio Watanabe

Retail Sales
Jan Rudd
888-225-9199 x12
janr@scrapbooktrendsmag.com

Subscriptions/Customer Service Sarah Dalsing

Shipping/Receiving
Clinton Herndon, Tina Gonzales

Internet Customer Service
support@scrapbooktrendsmag.com

Advertising
Amber Hall
888-225-9199 x14
amberh@scrapbooktrendsmag.com

Scrapbook Trends Magazine is published 12 times
a year by Northridge Media, LLC.
P.O. Box 1570 Orem, Utah 84059-1570
phone **888-225-9199** fax **801-225-6510**
e-mail: support@scrapbooktrendsmag.com
www.scrapbooktrendsmag.com

Subscriptions 1-888-225-9199
6 issue subscription: $49.95
12 issue subscription: $84.95
18 issue subscription: $124.95
24 issue subscription: $159.95
Please call for international rates.

Please send address changes to:
Northridge Media
P.O. Box 1570
Orem, Utah 84059-1570
or e-mail: support@scrapbooktrendsmag.com

Please send reader submissions to:
submissions@scrapbooktrendsmag.com

*Journaling is a way
of holding onto
the things you love
and the things you
never want to lose.*

~unknown

Laurel

Laurel is a sassy and sophisticated new line with an original color pallet and fresh, bold designs that you've come to expect from Scenic Route Paper Co.

www.scenicroutepaper.com

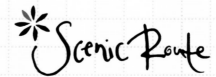

find inspiration & enlightenment online!

web exclusives / idea gallery / online shopping

Introduction

I RECENTLY REREAD A SHORT story by Alice Walker called Everyday Use, in which two sisters from the Deep South (one modern and educated, one shy and engaged to a farmer) both want the family heirlooms. The worldly Dee plans to show them off in her home as decorations, while the reserved Maggie simply loves them; she needs the quilts to stay warm and the churn to make her own butter. In the end, their mother gives the heirlooms to the daughter who will get "everyday use" out of them. As I read, I started thinking about my own scrapbooks. How often do I really get them down and look through the pages I've made, instead of letting them decorate my shelves? What is my true purpose in creating these books?

The answer came a few days ago, when my son Maxton got out one of his scrapbooks. As I listened from the other room, I could hear him and his older brother Xander flipping through the pages. I heard squeals of delight as they found a picture of Grandma, of Aunt Melissa, of Grandpa Henry in California. I had to laugh as they argued over an ambiguous photo: Was it Xander or Maxton as a baby? At that moment, all the work I put into my scrapbooks was worth it, because my sons know they have a place in this world that is grounded in love and they have people who adore them. It was my own prime example of everyday use.

Sometimes I wonder if we scrapbook simply because we feel like we have to—yet another chore on our to-do lists. I know I've felt that way from time to time. But I also know that scrapbooking is so much more than just another duty to fulfill. We are recording the history of our lives, leaving a legacy for our children so they will really know who we (and by extension, who they) are. Journaling is a crucial part of that legacy, one that is too often neglected or passed over. It's easy to understand why—coming up with just the right words or approach can be quite difficult and can prevent us from moving forward (there's a reason it's called writer's *block*). But journaling doesn't have to be hard, and it certainly doesn't have to stop us from getting to the heart of the matter!

That is what this book is all about: realizing what stories are meaningful to you, and finding ways to record them. As you do, you'll be creating something that is not only beautiful, but will (like a lovely quilt that keeps you warm) be used everyday to strengthen the connections between those you love. I hope as you read it, you will be inspired to expand the way you journal. Whether it's utilizing a new point of view, making a special mini album, or digging deeper into your own writing style, I think you'll find that journaling can be the most fun part of the page—as well as the most rewarding.

Kara Henry

Getting Creative

THERE IS A WORLD OF creative, compelling things you can do with the content of your journaling. So how come I feel like I'm always putting my thoughts on the page in the exact same ways? It's easy to stick with the same journaling style from layout to layout, but if you shake it up from time to time, you'll find unexpected insights and details that make your scrapbooks more fun—both to read and to write.

Ways you can get creative:

- Write from a different point of view—that of a child, a pet or even an inanimate object.
- Write a movie trailer or news report about the event you're scrapping.
- Challenge yourself to make a layout with x photos, a piece of cardstock, and some ribbon (or any one embellishment).
- With an idea book or scrapbook magazine in hand, have a friend choose a random number, then scraplift the layout on that page.

Turn to the end of this section for a list of supplies.

{ FIND WAYS TO USE YOUR SCRAPS. Not only does this method use up extra alphabet letters, but it's visually interesting as well. Using my own handwriting was an easy way to work in the words I wanted to highlight and helped me avoid the more complicated and time-consuming process of arranging things on the computer.

{ FIND WAYS TO FIT IT ALL IN. This is yet another page where I didn't have quite enough room for all the elements I wanted to include. The classic solution to a space problem is adding a flap for your journaling, and so I gave it a go. In this case, even adding a flap wasn't enough, so I allowed the flap to open to the back as well as the front.

"David, I've learned so much from you. Marriage has been more of a learning experience than I anticipated. I'm so glad we've had the past five years to learn and grow together and most of all, to love each other. These are some of the things I've learned – to think about things before I say them, (by example) to be giving and unselfish, to forgive, more about myself, to rely on someone else, to have joy, to be patient, to be open, that relationships are the most important things in life, it's ok to be wrong sometimes, to cry and be comforted, to feel safe, to laugh, most of all how to love without reserve with my whole soul."

{ UTILIZE THE EXTRA SPACE IN A PHOTO. When I took this picture of my cousin and my youngest son together, I loved it and knew it would need to be enlarged. But the problem I run into when using a big photo on my pages is that it often leaves little room for journaling. Here I solved this dilemma by adding the journaling (and some decorative elements while I was at it) in Adobe Photoshop before printing the picture. If you don't have access to an editing program, you can journal directly on the print with a photo-safe felt tip pen.

"It's funny that is doesn't seem that long ago that it was me with a little cousin on my lap, me who stayed home to babysit, me who spent hours entertaining the babies, learning to care for them, changing diapers. Now, those little girls have grown up and so have I. They do the same things for my kids that I used to do for them."

LOOK AROUND YOU FOR INSPIRATION. I knew I wanted to do "step-by-step" journaling for this particular page, but I felt like I'd been using strips of journaling too often—I wanted to try a new approach. As I was designing the layout, I happened to notice these office tags on my desk (I have hundreds), and it triggered an idea for getting those steps on the page in an original way. To accomplish this design, I typed my journaling in text boxes in a word processing program, arranged them in the document, and then printed a test sheet. I was happy with the result, so I used a light box to place the tags with temporary adhesive then ran the page through my printer again.

much fun out in the snow. His nose ran. When he touched the snow, his

dec. 2005

max didn't have very

hands got cold. He sat down +

his pants got wet. Poor little guy. He was so happy to go inside and

warm up.

chilly

{ MAKE YOUR JOURNALING A DESIGN ELEMENT. On this page, my words do double duty: they lead the eye around the page as a decorative border and also tell a story. To make sure it could still be easily read, I wrote clearly and a bit larger than normal. Try this concept if you only have a few sentences of journaling.

SOUVENIRS by Angela Marvel

In June, 2005, we sold our townhouse...the first place we owned...the first place we called home...

The only tangible things I have from the townhouse are these items, these souvenirs, as I call them. They are a collection of various objects that were spread throughout our home (and most even came with it) and are now all together in a special box. A box that will take them to their new home, where they will be spread out again and help bring a little bit of my old home to my new home.

I admit it. I am an overly sentimental person. It was hard to move out of our first home and leave that life behind, but I know that these little reminders will help the transition between the two homes and also help remind both Chris and I of special memories we shared in our very first home...the first place we owned...our townhouse...

SOUVENIRS

{ ON THE BORDER. I love the bold border Angela made using a list of objects that were meaningful to her; what a cool design element. Notice how her journaling is sweet without being overly sentimental.

MATERNAL INSTINCT by Kathleen Taylor

{ TUCK IT AWAY. This layout has it all—not only creative design, but journaling that is meaningful and rich with details. Kathleen wrote on a circle tag, then tucked it into a pocket on the bottom right coaster.

When you two were born, I was a bit overwhelmed. Being a new mom with twins, I did not know how to handle it all. The emotions, the craziness, the lack of sleep, all of it. But I did the best I could. A few months after you were born, I got a little depressed. Maybe 'depressed' is not the right word. I felt like something was missing. My friends had told me that when they first laid eyes on their children, they were overcome with love. A love they had never experienced before. I realized that is what was missing. It is not that I did not love you because I did, I just did not feel what my friends had described. I felt horrible like an unfit mother. I cried a lot those first few months. Then, in October of 2002, our area was rocked by two snipers. Two men that went on a killing spree randomly shooting people. It was horrible. I had to run to Target one day and as I pulled into the parking lot something came over me. An overwhelming need to protect you. I was petrified of the idea of harm coming to you. My motherly instinct kicked in big time! As I put you two in the stroller I made myself into a 'human shield'. I looked over my shoulder waiting to see the white van, the sniper's van. While walking to and from the store I walked beside the stroller. Keeping you between me and the parked cars. Once I got home I was relieved. The snipers woke up the mother in me. Looking back I realize that I had it in me all along I just did not know it. I was so busy trying to 'be' a mother, I forgot to take time to 'feel' like one."

{ INTEGRATE JOURNALING INTO YOUR DESIGN. This ingenious flap opens to reveal the story about how Lisa's family is adding a chapter to the history of their 80-year-old home. This is a great way to fit in lots of journaling on an 8 ½ x 11" page, and a fun way to make the layout interactive. Lisa took it a step further by designing the space underneath the flap to integrate into the whole look of her layout.

"This story doesn't start with us. It begins in 1925 when this house was built, and with the first family that moved in. A family that painted and decorated, that lived here and loved here, that made this house their own. It continues for 80 years, through all the people that put their hands and hearts and lives into this house, each leaving their mark before moving on. And now it's our turn. Our turn to paint and to decorate, to live here and love here. And while it's a central character in our lives, I know that we're just adding another chapter to the ongoing story of this house."

DREAM. HOPE. WISH. by Jen Jockisch

This is the
silhouette of a woman...
a woman pregnant with her first child
A scared, nervous, fearful woman.
So many things could go wrong.
Brad & I could screw you up
so many different ways.

Fate could intervene & cause
problems, things we have no
control over. So many things
can go wrong, some
inevitably will. But I think it will
all be worth it. Every minute
of fear doubt & worry will
hopefully be offset by the
most all-encompassing love we've ever
felt. We can't wait to meet you.
see what kind of person you will
become. Will you have your daddys
sense of humor, your mamas brains?
Will you inherit fierce insecurity from the
both of us? Will you be fickle
like Mama – steady like Dad? Lefty
or righty? Will you take mamas
creative beat, or Dads athletic one?
I'm sure you'll get the love of
books that we both have; just as
I'm sure you'll inherit our
fair skin, light hair & eyes.
But will you love the water
like we do? Will you inherit
mamas intense sense of
loyalty, Daddys extreme
dedication? Dads common
sense, Moms dreams? No
matter what you become,
who you are and –we will
love you. I'm sure of it.
Hurry up and get here.

{ JOURNAL IN UNEXPECTED PLACES. It's natural to worry and wonder about your child when you are pregnant. Jen used a photo of her pregnant profile as a journaling spot to write about her dreams, hopes and wishes for her new baby.

This is the silhouette of a woman…a woman pregnant with her first child. A scared, nervous, fearful woman. So many things could go wrong. Brad and I could screw you up so many different ways. Fate could intervene and cause problems, things we have no control over. So many things can go wrong, some inevitably will. But I think it will all be worth it. Every minute of fear and doubt and worry will hopefully be offset by the most all-encompassing love we've ever felt. We can't wait to meet you, see what kind of person you will become. Will you have your daddy's sense of humor, your mama's brains? Will you inherit fierce insecurity from the both of us? Will you be fickle like mama – steady like Dad? Lefty or righty? Will you take mama's creative beat or Dad's athletic one? I'm sure you'll get the love of books that we both have; just as I'm sure you'll inherit our fair skin, light hair and eyes. But will you love the water like we do? Will you inherit mama's intense sense of loyalty, Daddy's extreme dedication? Dad's common sense, mama's dreams? No matter what you become; who you are – we will love you. I'm sure of it. Hurry up and get here."

{ USE SPACE IN CREATIVE WAYS. Erica's journaling pulls out from behind her photo like a fan, then tucks back in, leaving just a black line showing. I love the crisp yet eclectic look of this layout, achieved by using black and white elements on her page.

"Wendell, you have always inspired me. I have learned what it is to be patient, what it is to endure. You taught me what it is to be humble and to be honest with myself. I've watched you grow, change and become this awesome man. I have learned words are cheap and it's okay to be wrong. Embrace life both good and bad and hold tight to what you believe in always. I love you."

I HAVE NOTICED THAT many of my pages chronicle the achievements and milestones of my children. When I started scrapbooking after the birth of my first child, Xander, I wanted to use his scrapbooks as a type of baby book. But soon I expanded it to include more stories and milestones, and it's continued to grow from there. Scrapbooking children as they grow is such a fun way to celebrate their lives! It is not only enjoyable and rewarding to the scrapper, but fosters self esteem for the child. Here are a few ways that I've recorded my children growing up.

More "growing up" ideas:
- A growth chart
- Teeth (getting or losing)
- Learning to get dressed by themselves
- Learning to read
- Accomplishments at preschool
- Games they like to play
- First time they spend the night at a friend's house
- Classes they are taking in school
- First date

Turn to the end of this section for a list of supplies.

Mason, you make me laugh. You're such a big kid. Maybe you're just trying to keep up with Xander. When we went to your two-year-old check up, your height + head circumference were 97th percentile + your weight was 90%. Sheesh, little boy, you don't look like you are two or talk like you are two. You're too big – stop it RIGHT Now!

97th

percentile

APR 1 8 2006

TRACK THEIR PHYSICAL GROWTH. I'm not very good at keeping up-to-date growth charts for my children. So I was excited when my doctor's office recently got a computer program that tracks their growth at each appointment; they even give me a print out to take home. How cool is that? Before that convenience, I did try to make layouts that tracked my children's growth at particular points. You can simply take out a tape measure every other month and jot down the info on a piece of paper you store in the back of their scrapbook to keep track until you're ready to scrap it. Kids love to hear about their progress and it will be fun to look back and see how they've grown.

These are the responses I got when I asked the boys what they were doing in these photos: **Xander** said, "I gotta a basketball. We're looking for something in that picture...

I'm staring, on the ground, an ant, not a butterfly." **Maxton** said, "Looking for ants. They on the sidewalk. They don't have cars. They have toes and knees."

bugs

APR 2 3 2006

{ GET IT VERBATIM. Sometimes nothing else shows the growth of a child more than writing down their exact words. I was pretty surprised at the responses I got when I asked Xander and Maxton about these photos. I was prepared to write them down, but if you want to transcribe it later or want a record of their voices, you could use a recording device.

Griffin, you got your teeth so early—Maddy and you got your molars at the same time. Your first teeth showed up at 4½ months. I was shocked. I knew you were teething, but I didn't expect them so soon. When your top teeth came in, you had a huge gap, which gives your smile tons of character!

{ LOOK FOR PHYSICAL SIMILARITIES. When Griffin's top teeth came in, I had to laugh. He looks just like me, with a huge gap in his front teeth. I'm sure we'll be looking at braces in the future, even if these are just his baby teeth! I haven't been too successful at getting them on camera though, because his usual smile covers them up. This photo was the perfect chance to journal about his teeth and about how soon they've come in.

JUN 15 2006

I couldn't believe it when I saw you climbing this tree in Black-smith Fork Canyon. Where did you get so sure-footed, so coordinated and so confident? I'm glad you couldn't get too far up, because I get nervous at the thought of you getting hurt. I hope I can keep it under control & that I will let you be your adventurous & confident self (within reason, however!) this is, afterall, just the first of many trees you will climb in your boyhood....

tree

NOTE WHAT THEIR ACTIVITIES MEAN TO YOU. When I saw Xander in this t
I knew that I needed a picture of it. He didn't get very high, but it was high enough to b
important accomplishment. I also took this as a chance to journal about my protective n
mother and how I hope I won't hold him back.

POTTY TRAINED?

Well, my first experience with potty training has been interesting. We started really trying to train you about three days before we went to Brett's wedding in Las Vegas. I wasn't so sure how that was going to work, but you did great! You went potty at the gas stations when we stopped to get gas and that was it. You've been amazingly good about it all. You loved getting stars and earning prizes and even without all that, you're still pretty good about going. Recently, when you have to go, you'll yell, "I'm gonna pee my pants." Then we tell you to run to the potty and you generally make it in time. There is one hang up though. You won't poop in the potty. Oh well, I'm sure that will come in time. I'm so proud of you and how big you are getting!

POTTY TRAINED?

Los Vegas, NV

APR 1 0 2006

...and no, he's not peeing on the tree!

{ GIVE THEM SOMETHING FOR THE THERAPIST. I've never been squeamish about sharing personal details. My son will probably be mortified that I did this page about him, but I'm still glad I did. It's been an interesting journey, this potty training thing, and I don't want to forget this important rite of passage.

new skill

Griff, you are so eager to start walking. We've actually started trying to get you to take steps sooner than Xander and Maxton, and you've done well. You still mostly fall down, but you've managed as many as six or seven steps in a row before, even walking on your own without any outside encouragement. It's pretty funny to watch you try to make it to the couch before you crash. I think if you'd just calm down a little bit, you could already be walking everywhere, but the thought of walking makes you so excited that you can barely walk at all. This makes me a little worried that you're not going to walk, that you're just going to RUN!

{ CAPTURE MILESTONES ON FILM. I'm sad to say that with my first two children, I really didn't get photos of them trying to walk. They were both over a year, and when they started walking, they learned quickly. Griffin was a different story. He was a little younger, so I had more of a chance to capture his cute attempts to take steps. This sequence of photos makes me smile and I'm glad that I finally got to do a "learning to walk" layout.

Within the layout:

MAY 2 2 2006

i love you

A few weeks ago after church when we were waiting for Daddy to finish with the young men, Sister Lewis (who is the wife of the 1st counselor in the bishopric) showed you how to say "I love you" in sign language. Since then, you will every once in a while make the sign and show it to me. It was quite a bit of work to make your fingers move like that at first, and your brow would furrow in concentration. If I sign it to you, you will silently nod, with a big grin, then sign it back to me. Then, you touch your hand to mine.

{ SHARE THEIR UNIQUE CONTRIBUTIONS. Sometimes I am surprised at the things that Xander picks up and then remembers for months. As the journaling says, this was one of those chance things he happened to pick up on that became a part of our family culture. Months later, Xander still makes this sign and I love it!

A few weeks ago after church when we were waiting for Daddy to finish with the young men, Sister Lewis (who is the wife of the first counselor in the bishopric) showed you how to say "I love you" in sign language. Since then, you will every once in a while make the sign and show it to me. It was quite a bit of work to make your fingers move like that at first, and your brow would furrow in concentration. If I sign it to you, you will silently nod, with a big grin, then sign it back to me. Then, you touch your hand to mine.

this was the first time we went to the park this year. Maxton was so BOLD. I could see some fear in his eyes at times, but he'd go ahead and do whatever it was that he wanted to do. He even used the big kid swings. Go Max!

3-24-2006

BOLD

{ FACE THOSE FEARS. I'm amazed at how much growth happens in such a short time. Maxton has always needed a lot of help at the playground, but this year he just took off on his own, no longer held back by his reservations. As a parent, it's rewarding to see a child overcome their apprehensions. What fears do your children face and how do they deal with them? This can be a great topic for a revealing layout.

DOCUMENT PHASES AND OBSESSIONS. What are your children interested in right now? Whether they are 1 or 21, what they love tells something about where they are in life. My boys went through a long train phase and I made sure to include this several times in my scrapbooks. On this page, I illustrated their different approaches to the train obsession. Maxton, the younger one, loves to take apart the tracks and make trains as long as possible. Xander likes the stories behind the trains and has picked up on the "factual" side of the obsession.

Lately, Xander has been drawing a lot. He will spend a long time drawing on his "doodle" as he calls it. Xander and Max have three between the two of them, so there is usually one around. He's getting pretty good. He will draw all kinds of people. I will usually have short spiky hair. Other favorite subjects are Daddy and Grandma. Today, he was drawing spiders. He knows that spiders have 8 legs, but he's not the best at only drawing 8 legs. He wants them to fill up the space!

AUG 0 1 2006

SHOW OFF YOUR CHILDREN'S ART. My husband and I both have artistic tendencies, so I have been on the look-out for any interest in my own children. Recently, Xander has started drawing pictures that are more than just scribbles. I loved this spider that he would draw all the time, and catching it on film was my only chance to document the impermanent magnetic doodle. Include your children's special drawings in your scrapbook. If they're an unwieldy size, try scanning (or taking a picture), and then printing at a size that works better.

Cardstock: Bazzill Basics; Paper: American Crafts; Rub ons: Scrapworks, American Crafts; Buttons: Paperposies.com; Brads: Doodlebug Design; Stamps: Office supply; Pens: Sharpie, Zig

Cardstock: Bazzill Basics; Paper, chipboard letters: Scenic Route Paper Co.; Reinforcement stickers, date stamp: Office supply; Chipboard, rub ons: Basic Grey; Ink: Tsukineko

Documenting the dialogue that took place in your pictures is a great way to do your journaling.

Patterned paper: KI Memories; Metallic paper: craft supply; Stickers: Making Memories; Pen: Zig; Paint: Delta; Cutting system: Coluzzle

Kara added some flash to her layout with the stars she cut out of metallic paper using a Coluzzle cutting system.

Patterned paper, stickers: KI Memories; Ink: Memories, Tsukineko; Date stamp: Office supply; Stamps: Green Grass Stamps; Brads: All My Memories; Pen: Zig; Frame: Heidi Swapp

Kara cut out just the tip of the stamped "t" on her background paper and attached the frame so that the tip overlapped the bottom of the frame. She also added dimension by wrapping strips of patterned paper around the edges of her frame and extending them to the edges of the page.

Cardstock: Prism; Patterned paper, fabric: Craft supply; Brads: All My Memories; Stickers, date stamp: Office supply; Rub on: Basic Grey; Ink: Memories; Font: Garamond; Stamp: Heidi Swapp

A large tag is a great place to write your journaling. If you don't want to write on a pre-made tag, print out your journaling and cut it into a tag shape. The "O" in "POTTY" is a rub on from Basic Grey.

Cardstock: Bazzill Basics; Paper, rub ons: American Crafts; Chipboard: Basic Grey; Ink: ColorBox; Acrylic paint: Making Memories; Scissors: Fiskars; Font: Jensen

Notice how Kara used lined cardstock, a chipboard arrow, and arrow patterned paper to create motion in her layout, a great way to convey all the motion of a baby learning to walk.

Cardstock: Prism; Patterned paper: Fontwerks; Stickers: American Crafts; Transparency: Hammermill; Chipboard: Heidi Swapp; Ribbon: Paperposies.com; Ric rac: May Arts; Stamp: Office supply; Pen: Zig; Font: Franklin Gothic

Kara created a unique border by cutting chipboard flowers in half and attaching them to the bottom of her pictures. Notice how she angled her entire layout for a fun look.

Cardstock: Bazzill Basics; Chipboard: Heidi Swapp, Basic Grey; Buttons: Doodlebug Design, craft supply; Punch: Provo Craft; Pens: American Crafts, Sharpie

Make a "bold" statement on your layouts by using brightly colored cardstock and a string of brightly colored buttons as a border.

Cardstock: Bazzill Basics, Prism; Patterened paper: Karen Foster Design; Stickers: Doodlebug Design; Staples: Office supply; Pens: Sharpie, Zig; Ink: ColorBox

Cardstock: Bazzill Basics; Paper: cherryArte; Stickers: Doodlebug Design; Flowers: Prima; Ribbon: Paperposies.com; Date stamp: Office supply; Ink: Tsukineko; Colored pencil: Heidi Swapp; Pen: Zig; Font: AvantGarde

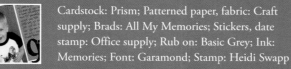

Relationships

Relationships are what life is all about. There is nothing more important to me than building and nurturing them. But relationships are complex and ever-evolving; therefore, not always the easiest thing to scrapbook! Yet I want to remember how things have grown and changed; more importantly, I want the people I love to know that I love them unconditionally. Scrapbooking is one of the ways I do that.

In addition to my own relationships with loved ones, I think it's important to document the relationships my family members have with each other. For example, I really want my sons to become best friends and so I try to foster that relationship through what I say in my scrapbooks. Here are just a few ways you can scrapbook the relationships in your life.

More relationship ideas:
- Record a funny conversation.
- Write about what you see happening in a relationship in the next 10 years.
- Document how two people are the same and different.
- Include your pets.

Turn to the end of this section for a list of supplies.

Griffin, I don't know if it's because you've been so sick lately or because I'm just getting to know you better, but this photo makes my heart melt. Little boy, I love you so much. Caring for you isn't always easy - there's 3 night feedings, medicine, & I've totally given up dairy, but it's all worth it, because

i love you

WRITE ABOUT CHALLENGES. By the time I had my third baby, I thought I would have the process of handling a newborn down pat. Then came the discovery that baby Griffin was allergic to milk, so I gave up dairy (no easy task). Next was a bout of RSV and a hospital stay that threw me for a loop, not to mention the normal sleep deprivation that comes with a new baby and the challenge of taking care of three children under three years. Although it was a tough adjustment, I really think these experiences helped me bond with my new baby and to have a deeper love for him. What challenges have you faced in your relationships and what progress have you made in overcoming them?"

m _maxton_

10

THINGS i LOVE about YOU

Your curiosity

Your affectionate disposition

Your strong opinions

Your funny, sweet and mad facial expressions

Your eyes and the soul behind them

Your independence

Your rough, little voice

Your love of music and dancing

Your intelligence

Your eagerness to please

{ MAKE A LIST OF LOVE. This is a simple way to let someone know how much they mean to you. I love doing these kinds of pages from time to time and seeing how things shift as relationships grow. It's also a good way to journal about those portraits that might not have much of a background story to go with them.

new baby
craddled in her mothers arms
as the morning sunlight
spills through the window,
Her father resting nearby.
Everything peaceful
after the bustle of the birth

calm

FEB 2 2 2005

{ BE A POET. Seeing my niece born was one of the most amazing experiences of my life. I was too central a character in my own children's births to fully appreciate the perspective you get from watching this miracle occur. As things wound down in the delivery room, my sister started nursing her new baby girl for the first time. Everything was so peaceful and the emotion in this photo is so powerful, that I wrote a simple poem to describe the experience.

Xander, one of the first things I noticed about your Daddy when I met him was his gorgeous hazel eyes. (Of course, that might have been because with a shaved head and a full beard, there wasn't much else to notice at the time!) You've got his eyes, from the exquisite shape to the long, dark lashes to the brown centers rimmed w/ green. You have such an expressive face, an innate kindness and sense of fun and it all comes out through

those EYES

JUN 10 2005

{ PICK A FEATURE. It's amazing to see my husband's eyes in the face of my oldest child. Not only do the two of them share physical characteristics, they have similar personalities as well. Both are extroverts, independent, kind. I wanted my son to know how much I love that he has his father's eyes.

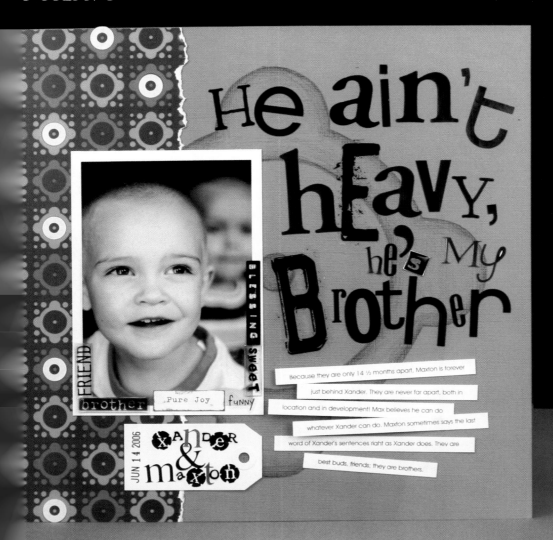

He ain't hEavY, he's My Brother

FRIEND

BLESSING SWEET

brother

Pure Joy

funny

JUN 1 4 2006

Xander & maxton

Because they are only 14 ½ months apart, Maxton is forever just behind Xander. They are never far apart, both in location and in development! Max believes he can do whatever Xander can do. Maxton sometimes says the last word of Xander's sentences right as Xander does. They are best buds, friends; they are brothers.

IT UP WITH A SONG TITLE. I've always loved symbolism and this photo seemed to volumes about my sons' relationship with each other. When we decided to have them so close her, I knew there would be challenges, but I hoped they would also be best friends. So far, it's d pretty well. After I decided on the direction I would take with this photo and wrote the ling, the song title just seemed to fit.

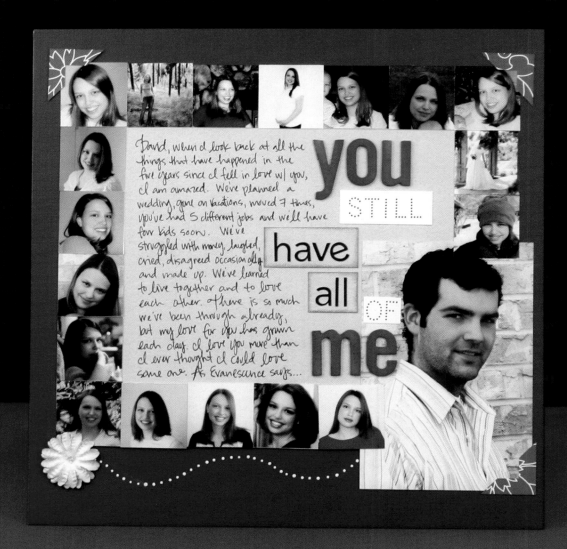

David, when I look back at all the things that have happened in the five years since I fell in love w/ you, I am amazed. We've planned a wedding, gone on vacations, moved 7 times, you've had 5 different jobs and we'll have four kids soon. We've struggled with money, laughed, cried, disagreed occasionally and made up. We've learned to live together and to love each other. There is so much we've been through already, but my love for you has grown each day. I love you more than I ever thought I could love some one. As Evanescence says...

you
STILL
have
all
OF
me

{ SING IT, SISTER. This layout was inspired by a favorite Evanescence song of mine. Although my situation doesn't exactly match the entire song, this particular line touched me and inspired this layout. Lyrics are a wonderful way to jumpstart your journaling—there's nothing wrong with using someone else's words if they describe how you feel (just give credit where credit's due).

2001

90days

from the day we met to the day we married.
6 days until we got engaged.
4 hours until we kissed.
36 days until we lived in the same state.
24 hours until we knew we would be married.
43 days until I met his parents.
20 days until I got my rings.
140 hours until we said, "I love you."
6 days until David met my family.
5 years later, still so happy!

ADD IT UP. I get a kick out of telling people that it was 90 days from the day I met my husband to the day I married him. It might not work for other people, but for us, it was perfect timing. What anecdotes about your relationship do you like to share? Was it the way he looked at you for the first time or the way you hated his guts for years? Use those little stories as a springboard for a layout. On this page, I had fun getting a new perspective on our years together by counting how much time passed between major milestones in our relationship.

Melissa is my best friend. My day isn't complete if we don't talk at least once. She just gets me

{ KNOW WHEN TO STOP. This is one of those times when short journaling is perfectly okay. This layout gets right to the point and expresses how important my sister is in my life. I was surprised when I sat down to do the journaling, because I expected to have a lot more to say. But when I didn't, I didn't force it.

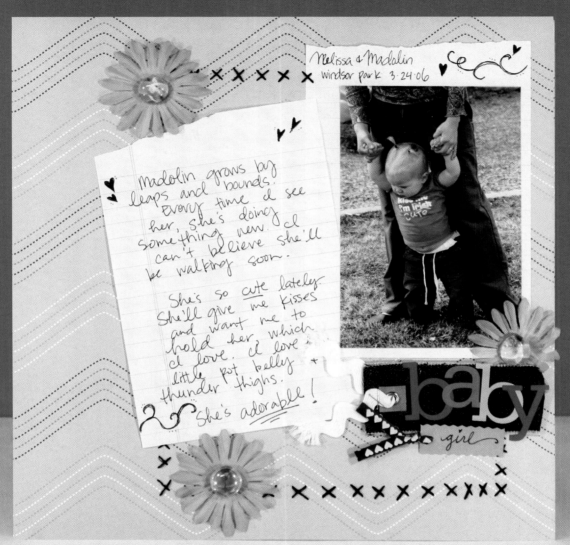

Melissa & Madalin
Windsor Park 3·24·06

Madolin grows by leaps and bounds. Every time I see her, she's doing something new. I can't believe she'll be walking soon.

She's so cute lately. She'll give me kisses and want me to hold her which I love. I love little pot belly & thunder thighs. She's adorable!

baby girl

{ INCLUDE EXTENDED FAMILY. Even though I see my niece quite often (at least once a week), it seems like she grows faster than I can keep up. I love to include her in my scrapbooks, because she adds a little femininity to my family of all boys and I want to make sure that she knows how much I love being around her.

NAH by Lisa Dorsey

LOVE ME

Right before Christmas there was a big snowstorm. The girls were playing outside when a skinny, scrawny black and white cat joined them. She looked so pathetic and hungry we couldn't let her stay out there in the cold. We prepared the girls for the fact that the cat may have owners that were looking for her but we also wanted to talk to them about the responsibility of having a pet. Greg took advantage of the trip to the pet store to discuss this.

Greg: It is a lot of work taking care of a pet.
Katie: We know.
Greg: You will have to help feed her and change her litter box. Are you willing to help with that?
Katie: Yes!!!!!

(Lauren's response was not quite what we expected though.)

Lauren: Nah...put her back outside.

Obviously we did not put her outside. After trying in vein to find her owners we have kept the cat, which we have named Doc. Lauren's feelings for Doc have definitely changed. The honest four year old who once wanted to "put her back outside" now adores Doc and is more than willing to help with taking care of her. You could say this is one time she is happy that we didn't listen to her.

to do list:
☑ feed me
☑ pet me
☑ love me

NAH

Meow   Meow

SHOW PROGRESSION. Lisa's layout about her daughter's relationship with their cat is b funny and touching. I like how she is honest about her daughter's feelings towards their cat Doc, and how she explains the progression of their relationship.

JuST uS

Have you ever loved someone so much that you just couldn't breathe unless they were near? A love that is so great that it **consumes you**... so that you are not whole without them. And I am not talking about any ordinary love... I am talking about the type of love where you hear him walk thru the door and your **heart skips a beat**, the type of love where you would give up everything you had for the rest of your life for just another moment with him... that type of love.

I do... I have this breathtaking, priceless beyond measure, **can't live without** type of love. I am so lucky to have found him and I thank God everyday. I can still remember the moment that I met him and I can't believe that it has been seven years. I told my roommate after our first date, "That is the man I am going to marry." We have spent the last four years as **husband and wife**, raising two beautiful boys. My eyes water every time I look at them because I can see my husband in them: in their smile, in their eyes, in their laughter. I can hear my husband in their voice when they say, "I love you too, Mommy."

It's hard to believe that my husband has been gone almost a month. He is serving our nation in Afghanistan and will continue to do so for the next several months. I think of him every minute of every day and I **pray for his safe return**. Lately, I find myself asking God to take back everything I ever wished for and saying that all I want is to grow old and spend the rest of my life with my husband.

Please God; all I want in life is **just us**...

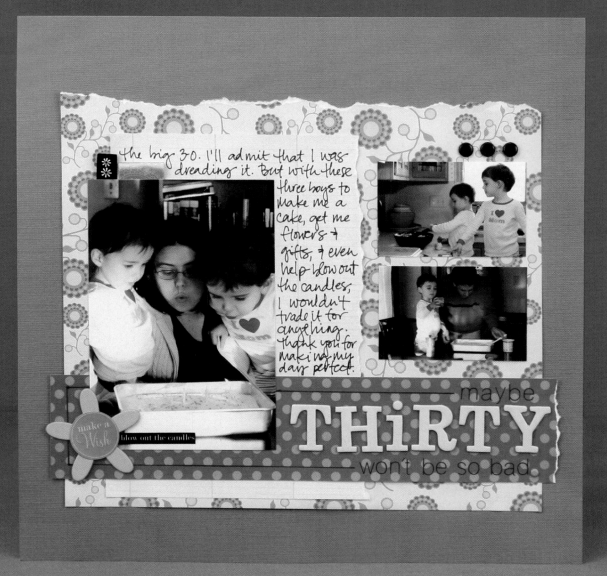

the big 30. I'll admit that I was dreading it. But with these three boys to make me a cake, get me flowers & gifts, & even help blow out the candles, I wouldn't trade it for anything. thank you for making my day perfect.

make a Wish   blow out the candles

maybe
THiRTY
won't be so bad

SEE THE GLASS HALF-FULL. Lisa focused her journaling on how her family turned a dreaded birthday into a day she enjoyed. I love how the event of her birthday framed the story of her relationship with her boys.

Cardstock: Bazzill Basics; Patterned paper: American Crafts, Pressed Petals; Chipboard: Basic Grey; Ribbon: paperposies.com; Rub ons: Scrapworks; Flowers: Doodlebug Design; Pen: Sharpie; Acrylic paint: Making Memories; Scissors: Fiskars

Paper, stickers, die cut monogram, tag: Basic Grey; Label holder, rub ons: Making Memories; Pen: Zig; Ink: ColorBox; Ribbon: Craft supply; Ric rac: Wrights; Font: Unknown

Notice how Kara used a tall, narrow picture to balance the horizontal lines of the journaling strips.

Cardstock: Bazzill Basics; Paper: Basic Grey; Ribbon, appliqué: Craft supply; Ric rac, rub ons: Doodlebug Design; Stickers: American Crafts; Pen: Zig; Date stamp: Office supply; Ink: Tsukineko

Kara used a calming blue color scheme and soft accents like the butterfly and flower rub ons around her picture to fit with the topic of her layout.

Cardstock: Bazzill Basics; Flowers: Prima; Stickers: American Crafts; Chipboard: Pressed Petals, Flair Designs; Mat: Craft supply; Pen: Zig; Acrylic paint: Delta; Date stamp: Office supply

You can create a title like Kara's by cutting up pieces of flowers and adhering them to chipboard letters, then flipping the letters over and trimming away the excess petals.

Cardstock: Bazzill Basics; Patterned paper: American Crafts; Tag: Paperbilities; Colored pencils: Heidi Swapp; Reinforcement stickers: Office supply; Stickers: All My Memories, American Crafts; Chatterbox, craft supply, Creative Imaginations, Daisy Hill, Doodlebug Design, L'il Davis Designs, Mustard Moon, Pebbles, Inc.

Try tearing your edges of patterned paper for a more textured look. Notice how Kara used different materials for her descriptive words around Xander's picture.

Cardstock: Bazzill Basics; Paper, rub ons: American Crafts; Flower: Prima; Chipboard: Basic Grey; Stickers: Craft supply; Paint: Delta; Ink: ColorBox; Pen: Zig

Kara creates a border of pictures of herself that goes all around her journaling and leads back to the picture of her husband. When layering with the same color of cardstock as your background, ink the edges to help it stand out.

Cardstock: Bazzill Basics; Paper: Flair Designs; Stickers: American Crafts; Pen: Sharpie; Shapes: Heidi Swapp; Brads: Making Memories; Acrylic paint: Delta

Kara painted the edges of her acrylic hearts to help them pop out.

Cardstock: Bazzill Basics; Paper: Chatterbox; Thread: Coats and Clark; Scissors: Provo Craft; Stamps, acrylic paint: Making Memories; Pen: Zig

The blue shades of the background match beautifully with the black and white photograph. Try outlining your stamped title with pen to help the letters stand out more.

Paper, stickers: American Crafts; Flowers: Heidi Swapp; Tag, pebbles: Craft supply; Ric rac: Wrights; Staples: Office supply; Twist tie: Pebbles, Inc.; Thread: Coats and Clark; Pen: Zig

Notice the way Kara created her unique title by attaching letter stickers to a tag made from denim and also how a twist tie is tied through the hole in the "girl" tag.

Cardstock: Worldwin; Patterned paper: Chatterbox; Metal embellishments: Eyelet Outlet; Ribbon: American Crafts; Tags: Paper House Productions; Crystal lacquer: Sakura; Staples, thread: Unknown

Lisa used American Crafts metal letters as a template for her title. Notice how she matted her picture, patterned paper and journaling for a clean, uniform look.

Cardstock: Bazzill Basics; Patterned paper: SEI; Brads: Making Memories; Chipboard, silhouette words: Heidi Swapp; Flowers: Heidi Swapp, Prima; Leaves: Prima; Tags: Rusty Pickle; Rub ons: 7 Gypsies; Ink: Ranger; Font: Century Gothic; Photography: Michelle Van Etten

Diana layered her photograph over blocks and strips of patterned paper with inked edges to help them stand out, while keeping the focus on the picture and the story behind it.

Cardstock: Bazzill Basics; Patterned paper: Fontwerks, Making Memories, SEI; Brads, rub ons, pens: American Crafts; Ribbon: American Crafts, Scrapworks; Chipboard: Heidi Swapp; Stickers: 7 Gypsies

Cluster your elements in the middle of your page, leaving a wide border. Bright colors and a few torn edges give this layout a fun, playful look.

Everyday Life

IN MIDDLE SCHOOL AND HIGH school, I used to do this thing I called the "Story of the Day." It involved telling some little anecdote from the day before, such as a funny dream I'd had, or the time I discovered my missing jeans were being worn by my little brother. (And no, he still hasn't lived that down.) During each new class I would repeat the tale to my friends; looking back, I realize it was yet another manifestation of my love of stories. Now as a mom, I've still got "stories of the day." They often work their way into my children's scrapbooks or my blog entries, and I love how these little vignettes come together to create the big picture of our lives.

More "everday life" ideas:
- The stores you go to in any given week
- How you spend your downtime
- A typical week's menu
- The routines you repeat from day to day
- The different rooms of your house and what happens there

Turn to the end of this section for a list of supplies.

This was the first time we took the boys miniature golfing where they actually got to play. They quickly understood the concept, but both of them refused to lets us help them learn how to hold the clubs or help them hit the ball. I have to admit, it was a pretty funny sight, seeing them swing the clubs way up over their heads, only to have the club stick to the green and they completely missed the ball. It was a long game, with a lot of un-intentional cheating.

Griffin was pretty content in the stroller, watching us play and taking in the scenery. This is such a beautiful course, sitting at the mouth of Provo Canyon. I can't wait to go again!

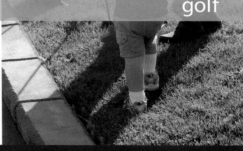

mini golf

4.25.2006

{ RECORD FAMILY OUTINGS. My husband loves to play miniature golf. Me…not so much. And while losing isn't usually my idea of a good time, on this day I gave in and we all went for a round at a local miniature golf course. Having my boys play was surprisingly fun, chaos and all. This is really a layout about having toddlers who refuse help.

MAY 1 1 2006

sun

shine

Madelin looked
so adorable in
her summer sun-
dress with the
light coming
through the window.

LET THE PHOTO DO MOST OF THE TALKING. This layout is one of those times when I just wanted to point out the reason I picked up the camera in the first place. Nothing too fancy, but the journaling draws your eye back to the photo to take a second look.

XANDER   5.23.2005   PROVO, UT

{ TELL THE BACK-STORY. Did I mention I love to take photos of my children while they sleep? This layout's journaling is a bit different, because I wanted to convey how much fun Xander had before he crashed on the floor. Even if you can't remember the exact details surrounding a photo like this, write down the type of things that typically lead to a nap, or the activities they do to unwind.

Xander, I can't remember exactly what we did this day that made you so very tired. I think we were over at Grandma Stephen's house. You play so hard while we are over there, and then often crash on the way home. This afternoon you managed to make it to the living room floor. No binki, no blanket or pillow, just carpet. I loved how the sun was shining through your blonde hair and the way your still chubby fist was curled up by your mouth. It's not a perfect photo; there's the bruise on your cheek from falling down at the playground earlier that week and some food on your upper lip, but you are totally at peace after playing your heart out. I love how you attack life with all your energy and then rest with a vengeance. You are my sun sleeper."

I'm sure you'll find this hard to believe boys, but I never pictured myself getting excited about trains, airplanes, helicopters and cars. As the mother of you two, soon to be three, boys, I find myself looking for them all the time. Dump trucks, low flying helicopters and train whistles are thrilling and so new, so full of wonder to you two, and I can't help wanting to help you find them. There is a lot of pointing and did-you-see-that's in our car and on our walks, and every time we see something mechanical and moving, we stop and watch until we can't see it anymore.

PLANES TRAINS & AUTO MOBILES

xander & maxton ~ july 2005

{ NOTICE HOW YOU'VE CHANGED. I was surprised at how, after having three boys, I have come to love looking for trains, airplanes and all sorts of cars right along with them. What surprises you?

"I'm sure you'll find this hard to believe, boys, but I never pictured myself getting excited about trains, airplanes, helicopters and cars. As the mother of you two, soon to be three, boys, I find myself looking for them all the time. Dump trucks, low flying helicopters and train whistles are thrilling and so new, so full of wonder to you two, and I can't help wanting to help you find them. There is a lot of pointing and did-you-see-that's in our car and on our walks, and every time we see something mechanical and moving, we stop and watch until we can't see it anymore."

sink BaTh

Dirty after eating? Nothing like a quick clean in the kitchen sink. Easy, convenient and cute!

{ MAKE A COMMERCIAL. When I was growing up, I remember my mom bathing my younger brothers in the kitchen sink, especially after a messy meal. Notice how the journaling here is phrased to imitate an old-fashioned commercial, which adds a sense of fun to the layout.

Each one of the grandchildren on the Stephens side has a nickname that begins with S. You are Squeaky. We came up with this one when you were just a newborn and I have to say, it fits. You are always talking and making funny noises.

SQUEAKY

JUN 3 0 2006

{ SHARE THE METHOD TO YOUR MADNESS. It started innocently enough. My oldest son somehow got the nickname Stinky, then my nephew became Squirt and Maxton was dubbed Squishy. By the time Griffin was born, we knew he needed a nickname that started with an S. "Squeaky" fit perfectly. Nicknames are so fun and personal; they definitely deserve a place in your scrapbooks.

FALL {DOWN}

On our way over to Grandma's house, Xander, Maxton and I stopped to play in the leaves on the lawn of the church. They boys jumped in this pile of leaves. I felt bad though, when I realized the reason they had all collected there was because they were covering a manhole cover. It's a good thing they are still small and don't jump very hard!

NOV 1 7 2005

{ TAKE OPPORTUNITIES AS THEY COME. Last fall, I wanted to take my boys out to jump in the leaves (and, of course, capture it on film). We live in an apartment with no big trees, so when I saw these leaves as we were taking a walk, I knew this was my chance. Notice how I included the detail about the hidden manhole cover, which adds a dose of "reality check" to the story.

"On our way over to Grandma's house, Xander, Maxton and I stopped to play in the leaves on the lawn of the church. The boys jumped in this pile of leaves. I felt bad though, when I realized the reason they had all collected there was because they were covering a manhole cover. It's a good thing they are still small and don't jump very hard!"

When we went to the park, I didn't realize that the drinking fountain was going to be the highlight of the trip. With all of our kids still 4 + under, it's pretty funny to see them trying to get a drink. I had so much fun snapping away, even if I was holding the faucet with one hand for Hyrum + Xander. I love how having little kids makes even the smallest task an adventure!

SEP 19 2006

{ DOCUMENT THE "LITTLE" MOMENTS. One of my favorite things to record is the unexpected delights of the everyday. On a beautiful summer day, my sister and I took all our kids to the park. After playing hard, they each wanted a drink. I happened to have my camera around my neck and so this layout was born.

LAUGH OUT LOUD

not an

INSIDE

VOICE

Our Little boy has found the volume control on his voice in a big way. It started with just a little yelp here and there ~ testing his vocal range. Lately, it's evolved into a full fledged SQUEAL. Kind of like a monkey. I am absolutely LOVING it though. The YELL means you are totally happy. Letting loose and having fun! The SMILE that accompanys the loudness is beyond PRICELESS to me. besides, we have plenty of time to practice your inside voice. Maybe we'll WORK on that once you turn two. I'M in NO RUSH.

Jason — 21 mos. old — April '06

OK ON THE BRIGHT SIDE. Katie tells the story of her little boy finding his voice
ch good humor (and a better attitude toward her noisy toddler than I can boast!). I was
wn to the vibrant colors of this layout, which perfectly complement the subject matter.

Aaja wakes up, goes back to sleep

7 Aaja wakes again, ready to play

8 I wake up. Mom usually calls.
I check email and nbs
9 Breakfast time + dishes

10 Aaja playtime. My project time

11 Errands or beach

12 Aaja goes down for nap while
I play or work
1 I need a nap.

2 Aaja wakes + eats

3 Aaron comes home for lunch

4 He watches tv & Aaja
Aaja eats again
5 Playdate with Austin

6 Home to eat or bath

7 bed time for Aaja

8 More playtime for me

9 Aaja usually wakes to
eat again.
10 Aaron gets home
We eat & watch tv
11 together.

12 Bed time.

Oct. 14, 2006

{ SCHEDULE. When my oldest son was still a baby, I made a similar layout about our daily schedule, and I love to look back at it and remember what a typical day was like. Athena's journaling paints a picture that will help her remember this stage of life, and will help future generations to know her better; I love the writing tablet paper she used to record their routine on this pretty layout.

Layout was created in Adobe Photoshop CS
Font: Myriad

Cardstock: Bazzill Basics; Paper, buttons, chipboard: SEI; Rhinestones: Heidi Swapp; Flowers: Prima, craft supply; Rub ons: American Crafts; Acrylic paint: Delta; Corner rounder: Creative Memories; Date stamp: Office supply; Pen: Zig

Notice how the painted dots resemble rays of the sun and draw your eye into the central photograph.

Cardstock: Bazzill Basics; Patterned paper: Gin-X; Ribbon: Michaels; Thread: Coats and Clark; Brads: Making Memories; Pen: Zig; Ink: Tsukineko; Font: Unknown; Label maker: Dymo

Make a photograph do double duty by tracing a big letter on it and cutting it out. Make sure you can still see enough to know what is in the picture.

PLANES, TRAINS, & AUTOMOBILES

Cardstock: Bazzill Basics; Paper: Chatterbox; Thread: Coats and Clark; Sticker: American Crafts; Chipboard: Making Memories; Letter Tiles: Paperbilities; Pen: Zig; Ink: Tsukineko; Font: Times New Roman

Stitching on your layouts can not only create flair and texture, but can really make certain elements stand out and stay put! In this layout, Kara used stitching as photo corners, to attach a strip of cardstock and to give her clouds dimension.

Cardstock: Bazzill Basics; Paper, rub ons: American Crafts; Ric rac: Wrights; Stickers: Doodlebug Design; Pen: Zig; Acrylic paint: Delta

Make a fun layout like this one by adhering vertical strips of striped patterned paper and horizontal strips of ric rac, then painting a dotted edge around your picture; notice how the lines create motion.

Cardstock: Bazzill Basics; Patterned paper: Fontwerks; Tag: Paperbilities; Die cut letters: Craft supply; Ric rac: Wrights; Date stamp: Office supply; Ink: ColorBox, Making Memories; Font: Quirky, from twopeasinabucket.com

Cardstock: Bazzill Basics; Paper, tag: Daisy D's; Rub ons: Heidi Swapp; Thread: Coats and Clark; Ric rac, date stamp: Craft supply; Eyelets: Creative Imaginations: Stickers: American Crafts; Pebbles, Inc.; Ink: Tsukineko; Font: GoudyOlSt

Patch together several blocks of patterned paper and photos, zigzag stitching over the seams just like a quilt. Leave an empty paper block for journaling.

Cardstock: Bazzill Basics; Patterned paper, coaster: Imagination Project; Ink: Tsukineko; Rub ons: American Crafts; Thread: Coats and Clark; Date stamp: Office supply; Pen: Zig

Kara covered a chipboard circle with patterned paper and inked around the edge. She cut it in half and used each piece as a dimensional border for her strip of pictures.

Cardstock: Making Memories; Patterned paper: A2Z Essentials, Junkitz; Chipboard, stickers, rub ons, paint, templates: Heidi Swapp; Stamps: Junkitz; Ink: ColorBox; Pen: Zig

Katie used Heidi Swapp acrylic letters as a template for the word "not" in her title. She cut them out from photo paper so they would be shiny.

ANOTHER DAY IN PARADISE

Cardstock, patterned paper, ribbon, chipboard, paint: L'il Davis Designs; Brads: Bazzill Basics; Paper clip: Magic Scraps; Die cuts: QuicKutz; Rub ons: Doodlebug Design, L'il Davis Designs; Ink: Stampin' Up!; Colored pencils: Prismacolor; Writing tablet paper: CCP Intl.; Photography: Aaron Patacsil

Athena lists the things she does in a typical day on notebook paper and attaches it with a giant paper clip at the top. Notice how she applied a rub on onto a ribbon for her title.

Everyday Life

All About Me

The best thing you can do on an "All About Me" page is be honest. Sometimes we have a tendency to sugarcoat the things we write ("I don't want my children to know *that* about me!"), yet the best writers put reality on the page unadorned. With honesty comes real meaning, not to mention understanding, so go ahead and lay it on the line, warts and all—future generations will appreciate knowing the real you. And if you want to keep a page to yourself for awhile (or indefinitely), there's no reason you can't have a separate album that is for your eyes only.

Some ideas for "you" pages:
- Places you've lived
- Your views (and why) on political and social issues
- Religious beliefs
- People who've influenced you
- Any kind of favorites (books, restaurants, movies, colors, people, seasons)
- The pets you've had
- Goals to accomplish by the time you're 30, 50, 100…
- How you've changed in the past 5 years

Turn to the end of this section for a list of supplies.

UNSURE

unsure

DEC 2 6 2005

It's funny how at 25 I still don't know what I want to do. When I was growing up, I wanted to be an author/illustrator for children's books. That still sounds fun, but honestly, I'm not good at writing fiction, and I'm not great at drawing either, even though I love to do it. So, when I started college, I choose English as my major. I have a passion for reading and a love of writing. I got so close to finishing, only one year left, when David finished his schooling and we moved from Idaho to Utah. At that point, I was so sick of English-type classes, so when I started going to UVSC, I decided against the English degree. I'd done a lot of it, I only had 3 classes left at BYU-I in my major requirements, and it just didn't seem worth it to start from scratch. I picked something else I had come to love, photography. Melissa and I took the beginning photography class together and I loved it. Everything about it. Printing my own photos was an unexpected joy. To get into the more advanced photo classes, I need to take some of the other visual communication classes. I took an introductory class that showed the basics of some of the Adobe programs. I found with my background in scrapbooking, I had a natural beginning in graphic design. I had found another thing I had a passion for. When I took the more advanced Photoshop classes, I changed my mind again, and decided to do a degree more geared towards graphic design. But since Griffin arrived, it got harder and harder to find the time and the energy to put into school. Life had gotten overwhelming; I was relieved when I quit. I love spending more time with my boys and more time being a wife. I sometimes miss going to school, and I know I will go back. Maybe then I will have decided what I really want to do.

{ WRITE ABOUT UNFINISHED GOALS. I truly love going to school and learning new things; so much so that I keep changing my mind about what I want to do! I used this layout to tell the story of why I haven't finished my college degree yet. I keep chipping away at it and someday I will walk across that stage. What goals are you still working on?

's funny how at 25 I still don't know what I want to do. When I was growing up, I wanted to be an author/illustrator for children's books. That still sounds fun, but honestly, I'm not good at writing fiction, and I'm not great at drawing either, even though I love to do it. So, when I started college, I chose English as my major. I have a passion for reading and a love of writing. I got so lose to finishing, only one year left, when David finished his schooling and we moved from Idaho to Utah. At that point, I was sick of English-type classes, so when I started going to UVSC, I ecided against the English degree. I'd done a lot of it, I only had 3 classes left at BYU-I in my major requirements, and it just didn't seem worth it to start from scratch. I picked something else I ad come to love, photography. Melissa and I took the beginning photography class together and I loved it. To get into the more advanced photo classes, I needed to take some of the other visual ommunications classes. I took an introductory class that showed the basics of some of the Adobe programs. I found with my background in scrapbooking, I had a natural beginning in graphic esign. Since Griffin arrived it got harder to find the time and the energy to put into school. Life had gotten overwhelming; I was relieved when I quit. I love spending more time with my boys nd more time being a wife. I sometimes miss going to school, and I know I will go back. Maybe then I will have decided what I really want to do."

JUST WRITE. This mini album is a fun project that can be completed in a day. I love that I finally got down some of my thoughts on various subjects—and that purse album by 7 Gypsies is too cute! Notice that I didn't use any photos; this sped up the process and also allowed me to explore subjects I might not have considered if I was just going by the pictures I had available. I stamped the page titles with VersaColor 92 Silver ink to add some glam.

I hate using the phone to call someone I've never called before. I make David make all the appointments. I took a trip to Texas from NY when I was 14 and my mom made me book it all myself or I couldn't go, trying to cure me of it. It took days and a lot of anguish for me to get up the courage to do it. I also didn't like to get ketchup at fast food restaurants

I was mostly an A student. My parents never had to worry about my schooling.

I'm not athletic. I wasn't naturally good at it and I never really practiced. PE was humiliating. There were two boys in my grade that would always tease me. I hated how unkind people became when they played sports and that sort of turned me off of them. After trying out in 7th grade for volleyball and being on the C team, I worked my booty off and got on the basketball team and the track team. But after that year, I decided it really wasn't something I was interested in (mostly because I wasn't naturally good at it).

I like Tall, Dark and Handsome. So, basically, David is my ideal man.

Additional journaling:
"SKIING – I learned to ski at age three, but now I'm a little scared of going down the mountain that fast and I'm super cautious. I can still do it though, even if it's been years since I went (not a good idea when you're pregnant and hard to do for a whole day with small children).

FOOD – I love to eat out. I would go every night if I could. It's a miracle I don't weigh more than I do after 3, soon to be 4 children and all the junk I eat. I'm also a candy/chocolate fiend.

READ – I'm an obsessed reader. I'm the kind of person who gets so into a book that everything else doesn't matter. I don't hear David when he talks to me. This is why I don't read all that much anymore. It's too hard to break away when the kids need something and I don't get anything else done.

GAMES – I love to play games, but I hate to lose. I pout if I lose. I've learned to keep it inside, but it still makes me mad and I ruin the fun for myself.

TV – Speaking of obsessions, I wasn't allowed to watch much TV at all as a child. We didn't even have a VCR until I was 11 (that would be circa 1992) and we only got one then because someone gave it to us. Before that, we used to rent movies and the VCR! Now, I'm a bit of a TV junkie. I don't do things halfway."

2004

I've always liked my name. It's Latin and means beloved or dear. My parents picked it because it's feminine, pretty, and a tad bit unusual. They also liked it because it was close to my mom's name, Karol. I'd only met one other Kara before I moved to Utah.

David & I have talked about naming a girl a similar name, if we ever have one. I'd really like to do that, but we'll just have to see.

Kara

{ HELLO, MY NAME IS… Names are a pretty standard "All About Me" topic and for good reason! Our names are integral to our sense of self. When you make a page about your name, don't forget to include the details of why your parents chose it for you, any history it might have (in your family or elsewhere) and how you feel about it. Other fun tidbits to include: your nicknames, favorite children's names, famous people with your name, what name you would have chosen for yourself, given the option, song lyrics with your name, etc.

I've always felt a connection to nature. When I was a child, my favorite thing to do was read in a tree. Mom left me once at the park, up a tree reading, and when she came back to get me, I hadn't budged from my spot or noticed that she had left. When I'm having a hard time sleeping at night, I picture myself in Blacksmith Fork Canyon, with the rush of the water and the hum of the crickets, and I begin to relax. I'm so grateful that Heavenly Father gave us such a beautiful place to live. When I'm alone and walking somewhere, I often notice the particular way a tree grows gracefully or the way the sun peeks from behind the clouds. Then I say a silent prayer of gratitude.

Photo taken in our backyard in Texas in 1993; I was 12 years old.

nature *girl*

GO BACK TO YOUR ROOTS. When I found this old photo of me climbing a tree, it brought back so many memories of my childhood years spent in Texas. I've always drawn strength and inspiration from nature, so it seemed a natural (no pun intended) time to express that in my scrapbooks.

I've wanted to try this for a long time, but I couldn't work up the courage. As I grew up, I went from blonde to dishwater blonde to light brown to medium brown + then just stopped there, at a dull, lifeless, boring mouse brown. I dyed it off and on since high school, but I've always gone lighter. I love my man's dark hair + with David coaxing me into it (he told me to go even darker than his!), I decided to try dark brown with just a hint of red. And I love it!

feeling

brave

NOV 2 9 2006

{ TAKE THE PLUNGE. Change scares me, so I'm glad I have a daring husband who helps my comfort zone. Without his encouragement, I never would have taken the plunge and d trivial as it sounds, dying my hair dark brown was actually a big deal for me—and I ended results. Try making a page about a physical change, whether it is weight loss, a haircut, gett new glasses; then be sure to include how the change makes you feel.

FINDING MY STYLE

finding my **style**

high contrast

Sucker for autumnal colors

mod is FAB

Can't get enough pillows!

bold yet pretty

love floral fabrics

When David & I got married, I really had no idea what I liked. I got hooked on Trading Spaces, maybe a little too hooked. I decided to take an interior design class as an elective. Found out I loved it, & even considered switching my major. I found I love bold furniture mixed with feminine fabrics and accents. I like clean lines & high contrast. Now, if only I could find the $ to make my vision a reality...

{ MAKE A COLLAGE. Doing this page took me back to those days of clipping magazines for school projects. (I always enjoyed that.) Making a collage can be a great way to define your style in any area, such as clothing choices or even the scrapbooking products you love. To make the picture more complete, I also included details about how my style has developed over time.

Can't get enough pillows! | High contrast | Sucker for autumnal colors | Bold yet pretty | Mod is FAB | Love floral fabrics

When David and I got married, I really had no idea what I liked. I got hooked on Trading Spaces, maybe a little too hooked. I decided to take an interior design class as an elective. Found out I loved it, and even considered switching my major. I found I love bold furniture mixed with feminine fabrics and accents. I like clean lines and high contrast. Now, if only I could find the $ to make my vision a reality…

I Will

1 I will be healthy
2 I will remember what is important
3 I will listen
4 I will love & forgive
5 I will make a difference

{ BE POSITIVE. Sande's layout full of positive affirmations is simple but very meaningful. I know too many times I get so caught up in day-to-day stuff that I lose sight of what I value; reminding yourself with a pretty layout like this will help keep you anchored.

I got the hamster for me, that's right, I confess, I used my 4 year old daughter as a cover.

I do not sort socks, if I HAVE to find a match I will look quickly, but I will leave the socks unsorted the whole time Tom is deployed, and ironically I will only wear matched socks.

I have stretch marks, ooh yeah baby, that's right, and some DEEP ones too.

I maybe scrub my kitchen floor on my hands and knees 2-3 times a year, I am a swiffer girl.

My bedroom is the messiest room in the house.

I always put the cap back on the toothpaste, however, I RARELY squeeze from the bottom.

There are so many "landmines" in my back yard right now I don't even want to estimate a number, but lets just say another dog isn't an option right now.

I am not selective enough and I will hang onto toxic relationships and be too nice because I hate confrontation.

I blamed the kids for the hamster getting loose, but really, it could have been me... I have no clue how the hammie got out.

I yell and threaten, frequently, especially to my poor husband who often did nothing wrong.

I have shrunk a ½ inch, but still tell everyone that I am 6'0 tall, I have no idea why, but I hate not being 6'0 anymore.

I thought I was a really good cook until I realized that my favorite recipes are all Michele's.

I cannot tolerate horrid children and will think bad thoughts about their parents.

I am freakishly sensitive about animals. I used to cry driving to post in North Carolina because there would be so many animals dead on the side of the road.

I am a happy crier. I cannot help it. I will cry at your wedding, I will cry at a girly movie. I cry when people are in love.

I don't dust my house until the dust bunnies actually start taunting me.

I fret about my weight, even though I only have 5-10 pounds to lose.

I am scatterbrained. I forget play dates, names, was almost 2 hours late to a birthday party

I am a procrastinator-just ask my dentist.

I am flawed, what can I say...

I AM FLAWED

TELL THE TRUTH. I have a confession to make. I would really like everyone to think I'm practically perfect…but I'm definitely not. And although I'm aware of my flaws, I admit to shying away from putting them down in writing. Courtney, however, is totally honest in her journaling for this layout—not only that, but she is able to laugh at herself, too, and the result is a very real, truthful layout that paints a more complete picture of herself. She's inspired me to do a similar layout and get over my insecurities.

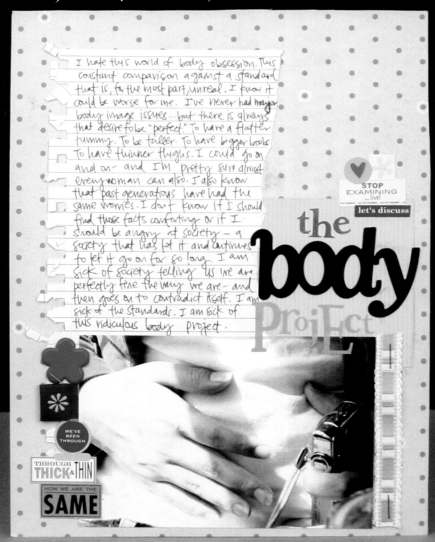

{ CONSIDER THE MESSAGE. When I read Caroline's journaling, I instantly related. She really got me thinking about what I agree or disagree with in the messages all around us—on TV, in magazines and on the internet. Contemplating media and our society can make a revealing scrapbook page.

"I hate this world of body obsession. This constant comparison against a standard that is, for the most part, unreal. I know it could be worse for me. I've never had major body image issues…but there is always that desire to be 'perfect.' To have a flatter tummy. To be taller. To have bigger boobs. To have thinner thighs. I could go on and on – and I'm pretty sure almost every woman can also. I also know that past generations have had the same worries. I don't know if I should find those facts comforting or if I should be angry at society – a society that has let it and continues to let it go on for so long. I am sick of society telling us we are perfectly fine the way we are – and then goes on to contradict itself. I am sick of the standards. I am sick of this ridiculous body project."

I've been thinking lately about how values are more caught than taught. I've been more conscious about acting the way I want my kids to behave. I say please and thank-you always and try to be kind to people. I've stopped watching mindless TV, because I don't want them to watch it. I don't eat junk in between meals and I try to eat fruit and vegetables every day. I read every day. I try to have a good attitude and be pleasant everyday because life should be fun! Having kids has made me...

A BETTER ME

{ WRITE ABOUT YOUR PROGRESS. Paula tells how trying to be an example for her children has made her a better person. I love the details she includes that describe what she is doing—how great that her children will know this about her!

My name Denise Levy
childhood ambition to be a politician
fondest memory time spent with my grandparents
indulgence CHOCOLATE!
last purchase set of golf clubs for Charlie
favorite movie When Harry Met Sally
inspiration my children
My life perfectly imperfect

7/10/2006

{ GET AD INSPIRATION. A credit card advertising campaign inspired this beautiful page
by Denise. Her simple answers are powerful, while the bright colors draw you right in.

Cardstock: Bazzill Basics; Paper: American Crafts; Date stamp: Office supply; Stamps: Fontwerks; Ink: Tsukineko; Font: Jensen

Kara cut strips of bright patterned paper, then wove them together in the middle of the page. This is a creative way to divide up your page, making sections for journaling, pictures, etc.

Cardstock, flowers: Bazzill Basics; Paper: MOD; Purse, mini album: 7 Gypsies; Ribbon: Paperposies.com; Acrylic paint: Making Memories; Pen: Zig; Punch: EK Success; Brads: Craft supply; Stamps: Fontwerks; Ink: Tsukineko; Font: AvantGarde

Kara created this adorable mini album to record her true confessions about herself. To keep the book uniform, she printed her journaling (including the border) on colored cardstock. Paper, flowers and stamped titles finish the pages. She covered the purse with matching paper.

Cardstock: Bazzill Basics; Paper: KI Memories; Rub ons, chipboard: Basic Grey; Rhinestones: Heidi Swapp; Pens: American Crafts, Zig; Paint: Making Memories; Ink: Tsukineko

To create her border, Kara drew a light line with a pencil to keep the painted dots straight.

Cardstock: Bazzill Basics; Patterned paper: Chatterbox; Button: Junkitz; Floss: DMC; Ink: Tsukineko; Rub ons: American Crafts; Fonts: Times New Roman, Unforgettable, from twopeasinabucket.com

Check out Kara's unique tag designs. After cutting out the tags, she wrapped a piece of torn paper around it with paper blocks layered in the middle. She then stretched floss through a button over the tag hole.

Cardstock: Bazzill Basics; Paper: KI Memories, me & my BIG ideas; Date stamp: Office supply; Rub ons: American Crafts; Photo corners: Canson; Punch: EK Success; Ink: Tsukineko

Kara punched small holes from her title to her photograph, leading your eye to a circle placed on her new hair color.

Cardstock: Bazzill Basics; Stickers: American Crafts, KI Memories; Brads: Making Memories; Flowers: Prima; Acrylic charm: KI Memories; Pen: Zig

Put all of those magazine clippings you've been saving to good use and create a layout about your style and the kind of décor you like. It's fun to look back on later and see how your tastes may have changed!

Layout was created in Adobe Photoshop CS2 Butterfly: Sande's own design, with some brushes from misted.net/brushes/misted.html and veredgf.fredfarm.com/vbrush/thearchives.html; Numbers: Rhonna Farrer (Old Stamps Huge Brush Companion set), twopeasinabucket.com; Photo frame: Rhonna Farrer (Split Pea kit), twopeasinabucket.com; Border: Sande Krieger (Borderlines), twopeasinabucket.com

Cardstock: Bazzill Basics; Patterned paper, stickers: American Crafts; Rub ons: Fontwerks; Fonts: Century Gothic, You Are Here, by Tia Bennet; Photography: Tom Kelly

Patterned paper, rub ons: KI Memories; Brads: Bazzill Basics; Ribbon: Unknown; Stickers: 7 Gypsies, EK Success, Heidi Grace; Fabric tab: Scrapworks; Velvet letters: Making Memories

Caroline wrote her journaling on notebook paper and embellished her page with phrase stickers describing her topic.

Cardstock: Bazzill Basics, Chatterbox; Patterned paper: KI Memories; Eyelets: Treasured Memories; Embroidery floss: DMC; Chipboard, acrylic star: Heidi Swapp; Rub ons: Basic Grey; Ink: StazOn; Font: Century Gothic

This photo was taken by Paula's 3-year-old daughter Molly. Notice how Paula inked the edges of a clear acrylic star to help it stand out.

Cardstock: Bazzill Basics; Ribbon: Strano; Chipboard: L'il Davis Designs; Flowers, buttons: Unknown; Pen: American Crafts; Twist ties: 7 Gypsies; Font: Times New Roman; Photography: David Levy

Notice how Denise added movement to her page by layering strips of ribbon as a page border. Make your own journaling template by typing it up in a word processing program and printing out on cardstock.

All About Me

Mini Albums

DELIGHTFULLY COMPACT, TOTALLY ADORABLE and chock full of fun. Yep, mini albums are the perfect way to tell a little story from beginning to end. Stick with a central theme, but don't be afraid to experiment with your writing style. This is your chance to step out of the way you usually journal and try something new—take a cue from your favorite children's book, unleash your inner novelist or simply let the pictures tell the story.

Tips for mini albums:

- Journal before you start.
- Incorporate bullets or lists.
- Keep the design consistent by repeating a page format you like; but do add some variation for interest.
- When appropriate, include a dedication page to explain the purpose of the album.
- A good title ties your book together—if you're stumped, try modifying the title of a book you like. (Who knows? It might even jump start your story-telling skills.)

Turn to the end of this section for a list of supplies.

{ BECOME A CHILDREN'S BOOK AUTHOR. My sister has made a tradition of sewing her children's Halloween costumes each year (overachiever, I know). In October, she and I got together at the fabric store to brainstorm what to sew and we finally decided on a fairy tale theme—her children would be a knight and a princess, and my three boys would be dragons and another knight.

Having a theme for Halloween lent itself really well to making a mini album, because the story came naturally (and the pictures were a blast to take). But if you don't have a theme, just have fun writing a story based on whatever your children decide to be. Snap pictures of them striking silly poses in their costumes to fuel the plot, then get your older children to help tell the tale—you'll have a Halloween to remember.

{ Your kids will love, as mine do, looking through a book that features themselves as the main characters. To give this story even more whimsy and magic, I added hand-drawn elements to the photos in Adobe Photoshop before printing them.

A FAIRY TALE

Once upon a time there was a beautiful princess named Madolin who lived in a beautiful country surrounded by mountains and filled with beautiful roses. She loved to walk in the forest and smell the roses.

One day as she was enjoying her daily walk, two blue and green fuzzy dragons blocked her path. Before she could say a word, they snatched her away.

They took her to a tall tower and made her stay inside. They never gave her lollipops. This made her very sad.

Every day the princess looked out at the surrounding forest, hoping that someone would see her beautiful blonde curls and rescue her.

After she had been in the tower for a long time, two knights went riding in the forest, hunting for food and having a great time together.

They saw princess Madolin up in the tower. They saw the fuzzy dragons. They decided to rescue her. They charged to the castle.

They fought the dragons bravely for a long time. The dragons were very strong and very scary. The knights almost gave up hope.

Then, all of a sudden, one of the knights had an idea. He pulled out a giant lollipop and told the dragons, "Let's stop fighting and all have a lollipop. Then we can be friends."

The dragons decided to take the knight up on his generous offer. They let Madolin out of the tower where she had been for so long. She thanked her new friends.

They returned Madolin to her kingdom and from then on, they were all good friends and they shared many lollipops together.

The End

ZOOM IN ON LIFE'S DETAILS. I'm not very good at keeping a traditional journal. (I aspire to someday.) So to make myself feel better about this, every once in a while I do a mini album that takes a more traditional, "diary" approach to telling a story and gives a really in-depth look at everyday life.

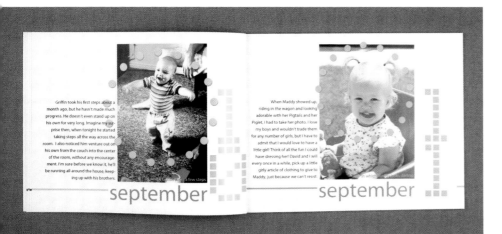

To create the album shown here, I took one photo every day for a month and journaled a paragraph or so to go along with the pictures. For the most part, I kept up the pace by making a page a day, but I did occasionally have to play catch up. To keep the project from becoming overwhelming, I kept the page design very simple, only varying the colors and the orientation of the photos.

This really gets deep into the things you do everyday at a particular point in your life. Even just a few months later, I enjoyed looking through this book and remembering all the things our family did, things that would probably never have made it into my regular scrapbooks.

{ BE DETAILED. In this fun mini album, Melissa uses short paragraphs packed with details to give a brief overview of her honeymoon, complete with small black and white photos to give a frame of reference. (Now I'm craving fish and chips!)

"It all began with vows. 09/02/06. COMFY – For our honeymoon in Halifax we stayed at the Halifax waterfront Marriott Hotel. Our suite had the comfiest bed ever! With a feather bed and a feather duvet it was blissful and perfect. We had some good sleeps. TUNES – Signal Hill at the lower deck. Jamie had been raving about this band and when we found out they were playing we had to check them out. YUM – The food in Halifax was super yummy. We went to the best little spots. Jamie was obsessed with fish-n-chips. I loved this chicken wrap with pesto and sun-dried tomatoes. SEE – There was lots to see and do in Halifax. We spent a lot of time walking around the waterfront. We also went on a brewery tour and checked out Citadel Hill. Such a fun, relaxing time."

EXPRESS YOURSELF WITH COLOR. Nancy used color to help tell how her family makes her life vibrant. She describes each of her family members as having a personality that meshes with a certain color. I love the bold look of her album and how the journaling is so connected to the hues inside.

The amazing cover was created in several steps. First, Nancy adjusted a photograph of herself to give it high contrast. Next, she printed out the photo and cut out the pieces to create a pattern, which she traced onto several neutral papers. She cut out the various pieces and adhered them back together on a red painted background to reform the original image of her face (notice the gem sticker for an earring). Finally, she embellished the cover with paper, buttons, flowers, letters, etc., finishing it off with a cool border made of paintbrushes.

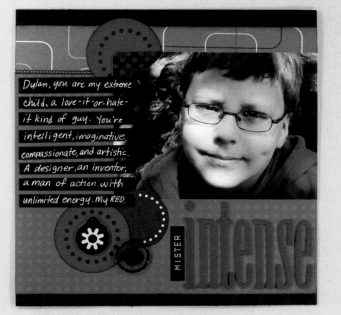

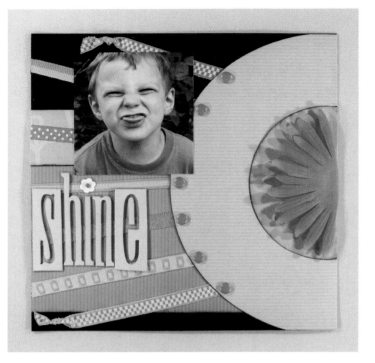

MY hero

Dave, you're a superhero, a man of many talents. Maybe not faster than a speeding bullet, but there's nothing you can't do. Your motivation and persistence and your love of the outdoors make you a "green" kind of guy. You're always growing, learning, improving yourself, and that is so inspiring to me. I admire you so much. You are a wonderful husband and father, the man of my dreams, and the love of my life.

CALM

POWERFUL

CARING

TALENT

SWEET

THE

sweet stuff

I'm an easy girl to please. I don't need diamonds or expensive toys to make me happy. It's the simple things in life that give me the greatest pleasure. These are the things that make life richer, deeper, sweeter.

K......ured at least one thing that happened to
h......family each day in September and created
h......digitally using Adobe Photoshop CS (she
h......ok printed online though My Publisher).
T......ttention to specific parts of her photos, she
s......d them with a ring of dots.

Melissa gives a quick rundown of her honeymoon in this cute mini album by using blocks of coordinating patterned paper, printed transparencies and embellishing with chipboard, acrylic pieces, rub ons, and a flower. She added extra interest by hanging some elements over the page edges."

Album is 9 3/4 x 8 1/2"
Cardstock: Bazzill Basics; Patterned paper, chipboard, rub ons: KI Memories; Brads: American Crafts; Flowers: Michaels (orange), Prima (teal); Buttons: Craft supply; Paint brushes, canvas board: Dollarama; Rhinestone: Westrim Crafts; Gaffer's tape: 7 Gypsies; Corner punch: EK Success; Ink: Memories; Paint: Folk Arte; Photography: David Davies

Let us put the spotlight on your work of art!

Interviews

WHEN I FIRST BECAME INTERESTED in family history, I sat down with my great-grandma and asked her about her life. At 100 years old, she has an amazing history; one that continues to grow. I thought I knew my grandma, but I learned things about her that day that I didn't know before, like how she used to take sleigh rides with my grandpa to watch basketball games and other fun stories. You can incorporate these kinds of interviews, with all the intriguing information they reveal, straight into your scrapbook pages.

To gather a lot of information at once, I planned a family activity especially for interviews. Each family member received a list of printed questions, with room to record their answers below. We then took a few minutes to think of our answers and write them down, and then went around the room and shared what we'd written. It was a great bonding time, with lots of laughter, and I got tons of information. You could also sit down with a list of questions and a tape recorder, then later transcribe your interviewee's answers later—this works great with older people or children, who may not be able to write as well. If you're really on the ball, print out questions on acid-free paper so you can put them in your books complete with the person's handwriting.

Possible interview topics:
• School
• Friends
• Holidays and holiday traditions
• Growing up with siblings
• Memories of your grandparents
• World events

Need help finding questions? See my Stories to Tell article in the December issue of Scrapbook Trends for several links to websites with helpful journaling prompts. Or you can download lists of the interview questions I used on the layouts shown here; visit scrapbooktrendsmag.com/idea_gallery.html.

Turn to the end of this section for a list of supplies.

What's your favorite color? Hummmm, red.
Where is your favorite place to go? Uh, to the park.
What is your favorite TV show? Incredibles.
What's your favorite thing to eat? Cereal.
What's your favorite thing to do with mommy? Counting and guessing the numbers. (Playing sudoku on the computer; I let him put in the numbers once I figure them out.)
What's your favorite thing to do with daddy? Have friends with him.
Who's your best friend? Griffin.
Which is your favorite shirt? The alligator one. (He was wearing it at the time.)
What's your favorite toy in the bathtub? The starfish and maybe the ducky too.
What's your favorite toy? My favorite toy is. . . Superman.

favorites

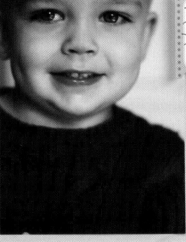

What's your favorite color? Red and yellow.
Where is your favorite place to go? Hassa's (Aunt Melissa's house)
What is your favorite TV show? Sporticus (Lazy Town)
What's your favorite thing to eat? Cereal
What's your favorite thing to do with Mommy? Play basketball.
What's your favorite thing to do with Daddy? Just play soccer ball. Soccer ball! Soccer ball!
Who's your best friend? Hyrum.
Which is your favorite shirt? I like turtles, but I don't like crocodiles. (Xander has a shirt with a crocodile and one with turtles.)
What's your favorite toy in the bathtub? Rubber ducky.
What's your favorite toy? Airplane.

SEP 2006

BE FLEXIBLE. I sat down with my four-year-old to ask him these questions, but my two-year-old wanted in on the action, too. I wasn't expecting real answers from him, but he had a great time coming up with responses and it ended up changing my whole idea of this page. Instead of a solitary Q&A format, I thought it was a fun twist to see their answers side by side.

What is your favorite thing to do with your grandkids? Play. Play. Play! Go on walks, play at the park, be in nature, jump on the trampoline and bound around house, read stories, play with play dough, sing songs, tickle them, talking with them, holding and snuggling with them, playing chase, laughing.

What is something special about:
Xander: His ability to learn. Always good manners and freely gives compliments
Maxton: Very tender heart, knows exactly what he wants, willing to share
Griffin: He enjoys snuggling. A bright countenance. Always learning and observing.
Hyrum: Full of joy, laughter, enthusiasm and very adventurous. Loves to draw.
Madolin: So adorable, tender and happy. Full of love.

Describe one of your favorite memories with your grandchildren. Going on a walk with Max and Xander to the "beautiful world." It was magical as we played on the hill. We rolled water bottles down the hill and I pretended to pull them back up with a rope.

What surprised you about being a grandparent? It was better than expected. That I could love as big as my own children and have only the fun part.

Take a guess as to how many grandchildren you'll end up with. 17

fall 2006

BEING
grandma

DOCUMENT FEELINGS. My mom spoils her grandkids, and I want my boys to enjoy every second of it. Recording how she feels about them and what she loves to do with them while they are still small was priceless to me.

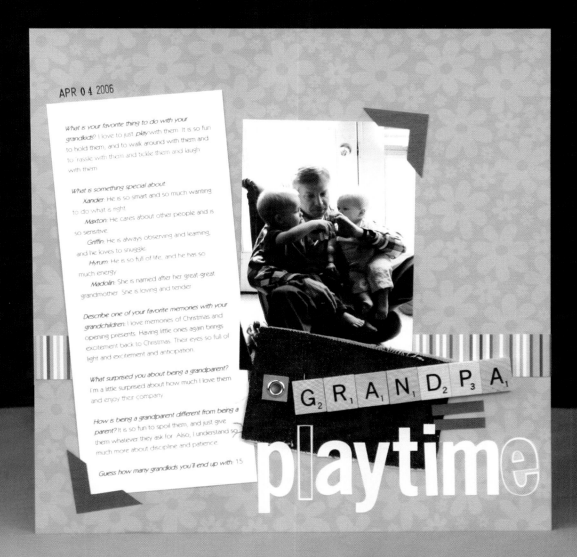

APR 04 2006

What is your favorite thing to do with your grandkids? I love to just *play* with them. It is so fun to hold them, and to walk around with them and to 'rassle with them and tickle them and laugh with them.

What is something special about:
Xander: He is so smart and so much wanting to do what is right.
Maxton: He cares about other people and is so sensitive.
Griffin: He is always observing and learning, and he loves to snuggle.
Hyrum: He is so full of life, and he has so much energy.
Madolin: She is named after her great-great grandmother. She is loving and tender.

Describe one of your favorite memories with your grandchildren: I love memories of Christmas and opening presents. Having little ones again brings excitement back to Christmas. Their eyes so full of light and excitement and anticipation.

What surprised you about being a grandparent? I'm a little surprised about how much I love them and enjoy their company.

How is being a grandparent different from being a parent? It is so fun to spoil them, and just give them whatever they ask for. Also, I understand so much more about discipline and patience.

Guess how many grandkids you'll end up with: 15

GRANDPA
playtime

{ USE AN UNEXPECTED PHOTO. Even though it may be a fairly formal interview, don't feel restricted to formal portraits. Try using a candid shot that illustrates an answer, like I did with this photo that shows my dad playing with his grandkids. (These are the same questions I asked my mom on the previous layout, but of course my dad deserves his own page, too!)

What do you enjoy most about being a Mom? I just love watching them grow. They are each so unique and interesting. I get a love of joy out of my relationships with my children.

What personal challenges do you face? I've never liked to be interrupted in what I'm doing. Learning to change gears quickly has been a challenge for me. I also get frustrated with the mess and I could be more consistent with discipline.

What is different from what you expected? I didn't realize I would get so much joy, even over the little things, like the look on their faces when I sing to them or the pride I feel at their accomplishments.

What do you get the most satisfaction from? Just taking care of them and teaching them. I love making them happy.

Why did you want to become a parent? Honestly, because I can't imagine it any other way. I've always wanted to me a mom and there is no greater work I can imagine than raising my children to serve the Lord and to be good members of society.

How did you decide the time was right? It just felt right. The thought of getting pregnant the first time was so exciting, I couldn't stand to wait anymore.

What did you feel after the birth of your first child? I was so tired. Xander kept me up most of the night after he was born. However, there was a moment when I was holding him, and I looked at that sweet face, so dependent on me, so innocent, and I fell in love. It was nearly instant. I would do anything for my children. I was so overwhelmed with that love, it was more powerful than I expected.

What is a particular memory you have about each child?

Xander: I remember going to Lake Powell when he was 6 months old. He charmed everyone who came on that trip. He never cried. He ate watermelon with gusto. He fell over in the sand. He did the motions to "Twinkle, Twinkle Little Star." He also had this way of waving whenever he caught someone's eye—he'd just stick his hand straight up into the air. That really sums up his personality; he is friendly, outgoing, smart and goofy.

Maxton: He's always been a bit prone to accidents. He gets too eager and doesn't watch what he is doing, but somehow it's a bit more than that. For instance, once I was carrying him down the stairs when we lived with my parents and there was a baby gate at the top of the stairs. As I went over it, my foot caught and we both tumbled down the stairs. Somehow I managed to protect him, and I ended up with the bruises. Scared him pretty bad though. Things like that just happen to Max. He was also the sweetest baby, giving kisses at six months and talking so much all the time. He has an ear for language.

Griffin: One memory that sticks out for Griffin is the time we spent in the hospital when he had RSV. I spent two days with him, nearly one on one the whole time. I was so worried about him. I knew he'd be okay, but it was still hard with him hooked up to everything and the doctors all concerned. I really grew to have a deep love for him during that stay. I also have to laugh at how much he thinks he is as big as his brothers. He also does this screaming thing, which is not very fun, but still a bit funny. If he doesn't get his way, he just lets out ear-piercing screams. It's pretty effective. He's also the most snuggly of the three—he will just rest his head on your shoulder. Melts my heart.

MOTHERHOOD

INTERVIEW YOURSELF. After I penned these questions, I spent some time really thinking a my responses before answering. You may feel a little odd asking yourself questions, but it's actua a great way to dig deep into your thoughts and feelings. I felt like these questions brought some emotions and memories to mind that were previously missing from our scrapbooks.

Q&A

with a 3 yr. old

Kaden's view of Me.

1. Something Mom always says to you?
   Broken House
2. What makes Mom happy?
   Balloons & Kaden
3. What makes Mom sad?
   Boo boos
4. What is Mom really good at?
   Pancakes
5. What is Mom's favorite food?
   Cereal

*this was a hard conversation. All Kaden wants to talk about is Thomas the train. ☺

March 2006

{ ADD BEHIND-THE-SCENES INSIGHT. Karen couldn't help but annotate her interview with her 3-year-old, explaining what he really wanted to talk about. That little note says so much about her son right now. Including a current picture of both the interviewer and interviewee is a nice touch.

how wonderful life is while you're in the world. elton john

Recently Pat and I celebrated our 15th wedding anniversary. It seems like a good time to reflect. So I interviewed Pat.
Terri: What are your thoughts when looking at this picture?
Pat: Where has all that time gone? It seems like yesterday.
Did you imagine us being married for 15 years? Of course.
What have you learned over this time about marriage? It is all about compromise and learning from each other. What is next for us?

lean upon me, i'll lean upon you, we'll be ok. dave matthews

i live for those who love me, for those who know me true. george linnaeus banks

and new phases of our life.

15 years

DREAM

GROW

Love This Life

{ TALK ABOUT THE PAST. This layout caught my eye because of its fun design. I also liked how Terri set up the interview, with her and her husband looking back together on the early years of their relationship. It's simple and sweet.

my new york soul mate.

Where have you never been in NYC that you'd like to go?
I'd love to walk across the Brooklyn Bridge because it's my most
favorite bridge in the whole world and I've never been on it. And
I've never been to Brooklyn before.

What is your favorite "tourist" destination?
Rockefeller Center. Especially in the winter when the ice rink
is open. So romantic.

Where is your favorite place to shop in NYC?
H&M. I love that store. I wish we had one here.

Where is your favorite place in NYC?
Central Park. I love to people watch, walk around or take a
carriage ride through it. Love it.

What is your favorite restaurant in NYC?
Serendipity 3. I love the ambiance of it--so whimsical and full
of stories. Not to mention yummy food and the fantastic (and famous)
Frrrozen Hot Chocolate.

What is your favorite non-tourist destination?
The Upper West Side. You won't find a lot of tourists up there
so it's a lot quieter. Plus that's where "You've Got Mail" was
filmed so for me it's a must see.

Most memorable NYC moment?
It's a toss up between skating at Rockefeller Center the day
before the tree was lit and going to see "Regis & Kelly." Both were
totally cool and very memorable.

Favorite new yorker?
My future husband. Ha ha ha.

A couple Q's from me and A's from my Sare
about our favorite topic... NYC!

I ♥ NY

Why do you love NYC?
I love the feel of the city--always moving and changing. I love
the culture. I love the artsy feel. I love the history. I love
that so much goes on in that small little island.

{ FOCUS ON A PLACE. Kelly's questions for her friend center around New York City and how she feels about it; her favorite places, etc. Getting someone's perspective on the city, state, or country in which they live is a unique, yet telling way to delve into their personality. I also love the fun title!

95

Danielle LaFave

age 23 | full-time student, scrapbooker, girlfriend to Dave | Mesa AZ

WHAT MAKES YOU LAUGH?
Singing + dancing with Dave.

WHAT'S YOUR FAVORITE POSSESSION?
my new camera.

WHAT SUPERHUMAN POWER WOULD YOU MOST WANT TO HAVE?
flying. I do it all the time in my dreams.

WHAT DID YOU WANT TO BE WHEN YOU WERE LITTLE?
a lawyer. That never really worked out.

WHAT'S YOUR MOTTO?
learn to laugh at life. No worries.

WHAT WOULD YOU DO WITH $1,000 IN SPARE CASH?
VACATION. More specific a Cruise.

WHAT'S YOUR SIMPLEST PLEASURE?
Sunday mornings with Dave, Lou. + Trix.

WHAT WOULD YOUR "I'D RATHER BE..." BUMBER STICKER SAY?
right now... In Michigan.

WOULD YOU RATHER BE A LITTLE SMARTER OR A LITTLE SEXIER?
Am I allowed to pick both?

THE BIG DECISION I'M CURRENTLY WRESTLING WITH IS...
Where to go after graduating this summer.

10.19.06

{ MAKE IT PLAYFUL. My favorite part about Danielle's layout, besides the fun and relaxed tone she has when answering the questions, is that she used her own handwriting. This helps differentiate between the questions and her answers, and also adds a personal touch. What a fun photo and a perfect match for this interview!

Cardstock: Bazzill Basics; Paper, stickers: SEI; Font: Futura; Buttons: Doodlebug Design; Date stamps: Office supply; Ink: Tsukineko; Pen: Zig

Kara made the focus of her page the interviews she had with her sons about their favorites. She laid them out next to their pictures and added name tabs and coordinating green buttons.

Cardstock: Bazzill Basics; Paper: Scenic Route Paper Co.; Rub ons: American Crafts, Doodlebug Design; Flowers: Making Memories; Chipboard: Flair Designs; Brads: All My Memories; Ink: Memories: Pen: Zig; Font: Jensen

For extra-special layout ideas, interview your parents or in-laws about life as a grandparent. Display each of their responses on pages with a girly or more masculine color scheme. Use striking accents like the chipboard swirl Kara used on this layout about being grandma.

Cardstock: Bazzill Basics; Paper: KI Memories; Stickers: American Crafts; Tiles: EK Success; Tag: Creative Imaginations; Date stamp: Office supply; Ink: Tsukineko; Font: Kabel

Try cutting out the middle of some of the letters in your title like Kara did to create a different and fun look. Keep game tiles from EK Success in mind when you have a game-themed layout.

Cardstock: Bazzill Basics; Paper: Flair Designs, craft supply; Brad: Making Memories; Ric rac: Doodlebug Design; Label maker: Dymo; Ink: Memories; Font: Garamond; Photography: David Henry

Dimensional label makers are hard to come by! Check your local craft or office supply to see if you can snatch one up before the digital label maker takes over. They make great journaling strips and titles.

Cardstock: Bazzill Basics; Patterned paper, chipboard: Arctic Frog; Brads, ribbon: Making Memories; Flowers: Prima; Stickers: Gin-X; Pens, corner rounder: Creative Memories

Cardstock: Prism; Patterned paper: American Traditional Designs; Ribbon: Craft supply; Stickers: 7 Gypsies, American Crafts, American Traditional Designs; Pens: Micron; Circle frame: Heidi Swapp

Terri cut out the round part of the design from patterned paper and cut it in half vertically. She then outlined half of it for the journaling and used the other half on the page.

Cardstock: American Crafts, Bazzill Basics; Patterned paper: American Crafts, Sassafras Lass; Brads: American Crafts; Chipboard: Heidi Swapp; Font: SP Chicken Noodle Soup, from scrapsupply.com

Kelly recorded her "Q & A" session on strips of cardstock with inked edges and fastened them with brads on the right edge.

Cardstock: Bazzill Basics; Patterned paper, rub ons: Chatterbox; Chipboard: Basic Grey; Rhinestones: Making Memories; Stamps: Simply Seasonal; Ink: ColorBox; Paint: Folk Arte; Pens: Sharpie; Font: Futura Lt; Photography: Marlana LaFave

Creating your own interview is a great way to tell about yourself. Notice how Danielle applied her rub ons right over her picture to help blend it into her profile.

Humorous

SALMA HAYEK, ONE OF MY FAVORITE actresses, has been quoted as saying, "Life is tough, and if you have the ability to laugh at it, you have the ability to enjoy it." I have to agree with her. I get a lot of enjoyment out of laughing at myself, but more than that, I love to laugh at all the funny things life brings. And with three little kids, there is something silly and delightful every day! Here are a few layouts that record some of the humorous things that have happened in my life; hopefully they'll get you thinking about your own funny moments.

Tips for humorous journaling:
- Don't over-explain.
- Let the photos help with the funny parts.
- Write as if telling the story to a friend.
- Don't be afraid to be informal; humor is rarely stiff.
- Pair the unexpected. Sometimes a serious photo can play off of humorous journaling and vice versa.
- Pay attention to the title—sometimes it works great as a punchline.

Turn to the end of this section for a list of supplies.

a conversation on

Xander: (crying) Ouchie! I got a ouchie. Baby, come kiss it better.
Mom: (Glad she doesn't have to get up) Maxton, go give Xander kisses.
Maxton: (Goes into their bedroom)
Xander: Baby, I got ouchies right there. Kiss it better?
Mom: (Still hoping she won't have to get up) Give Xander kisses.
Xander: No, right there. I got ouchie on hand. No, Baby, no bite!
Maxton: Okay.
Xander: No, right there. . . . Good job, Baby, you did it!
Mommy, Baby kiss it better!
Mom: Good job, Max; way to go!
Maxton: (Giggles) Boys - you are so silly, so cute & so sweet!

OUCHIES

July 13, 2005

{ BE A FLY ON THE WALL. When I overheard this conversation, Xander was a little over two-and-a-half and Maxton was barely 18 months. It still makes me smile and laugh a little at how tender and sweet it was. I wrote it down right away, since I knew I would want this funny story in our scrapbooks.

march 2005

self portrait

Xander, you brought me this index card and said, "That Xander." I was so proud of your first self-portrait. Dare I hope you'll be artistic? Still, I wonder exactly how many eyes you think you have.

POKE (A LITTLE) FUN. Sometimes a humorous approach can save a page from the journaling blahs. I had planned to use a straight this-is-Xander's-first-self-portrait approach on this page, but when I started talking about the drawing with my husband, I was tempted to put in one little sardonic remark at the end. (I really was impressed with his drawing skills, though.) I still laugh when I read it.

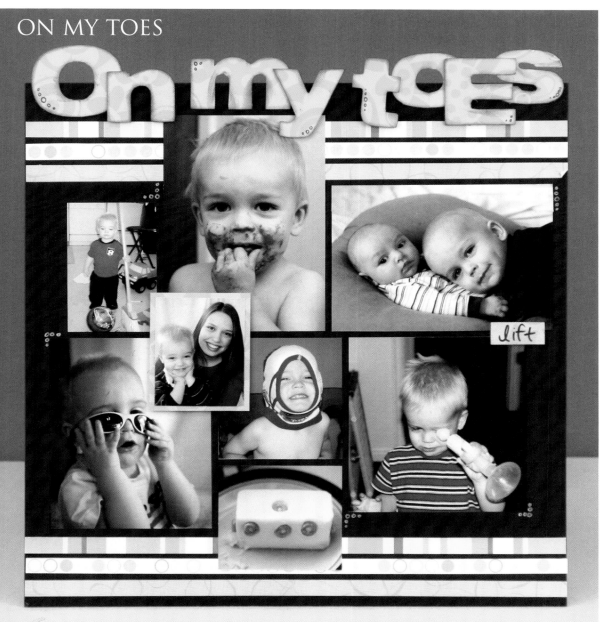

On my toes

lift

DOCUMENT THE SLAPSTICK. There are days when it's hard being a mom. This layout reminds me of why I should laugh instead of yell when my kids get "creative" with their messes. I just have to shake my head at the crazy things they come up with! What funny things do your kids do?

Journaling: Three boys are an adventure. They surprise me everyday with the things they do. They are so gosh-darn creative (see butter photo). They are mischievous—one morning they got into some pudding a neighbor had dropped by before I got out of bed (see Maxton covered in pudding. There was also pudding on the TV, the couch, the baby swing and the toilet handle, among other places). They are sweet (see snuggling photo). They try hard to be good (see photo of Xander sweeping). They are creative (see photo of Max using my breast pump as a "spy scope"). They keep me on my toes and they keep me laughing. There is no food they will not finger paint with. There is no game they do not like to play. There is no furniture they will not climb, no wrapped present they will not jump on and no candy that they cannot find (again, see Maxton covered in pudding, eating a skittle he found on the floor). There is also no photo they will not attempt to ruin (see pen marks on the photo of Xander in sunglasses) and no underwear they will not wear—on their heads that is. These are my boys. This is my life—always on my toes.

5-10-2006

unauthorized
FOOD

Oh yes, this is what happens if you leave Griffin in his highchair with Maxton's food nearby. Little boy, you are not quite
ready for table food, no matter what Maxton thinks! Luckily,
the meatballs ended up in your lap, not your mouth.

{ FOOD CAN BE FUNNY. Griffin likes to sit in his highchair where he can see the
action. When this mess happened, I had only turned my back for a second and yep, he
had food everywhere! I had to laugh a little bit and ran to get my camera.

Journaling: Oh yes, this is what happens if you leave Griffin in his highchair with Maxton's food nearby. Little boy, you are not quite ready for table food, no matter what Maxton thinks! Luckily, the meatballs ended up in your lap, not your mouth.

2-10-2006

A lot of people say that it's harder to deal with three-year-olds than two-year-olds. And while I can see their point (you certainly are strong-willed and independent), I have to say that I LOVE three. All of a sudden, you are so affectionate. You give hugs and kisses with abandon & you tell me that you love me all the time. I really love that I get to see more of this hilarious...

KISSY FACE

{ TELL ABOUT A FACIAL EXPRESSION. This photo cracks me up! Xander is always making funny faces at the camera and so I took this opportunity to journal about how affectionate he has gotten lately. If you get a shot of a silly face, think about a story the photo could represent.

Sometimes it's hard to figure out where to put you when you don't sit up yet. So, you get stuck in laundry baskets and couch corners. It's pretty adorable.

Feb. 1, 2006

{ CAPTURE THE MOMENT ON FILM. I love these types of photos. I think I have a picture of each of my boys in a basket of laundry. It's just too adorable to resist. The photo is funny all by itself, so my journaling was kept to a minimum.

Oh no! My CAMERA broke.

When I first saw these pictures, I was going to tell the story of how Mom and Michelle enjoyed spending time in the hands-on section of the aquarium. Then I saw something in one of the photos that changed my mind. On the first day of our trip, mom dropped her digital camera and the zoom would not work. We went to the PX and she picked up a very cheap 35 mm camera. She used the camera for a couple of days, but sometime during our trip to the aquarium she realized that the camera was not working. We didn't think much of it. The camera didn't cost much, so we chalked it up to that. Fast forward a couple more days and I download my pictures to give to Scott. I come across the photo that shows Mom's camera in the water and busted out laughing. I showed the rest of the family and we all had a good laugh at Mom's expense. Sorry, Mom!

{ IT ALL MAKES SENSE NOW. Have you ever caught something on film that you didn't notice at the time? Amy was lucky enough to catch the cause of her mother's broken camera and it makes for a great read.

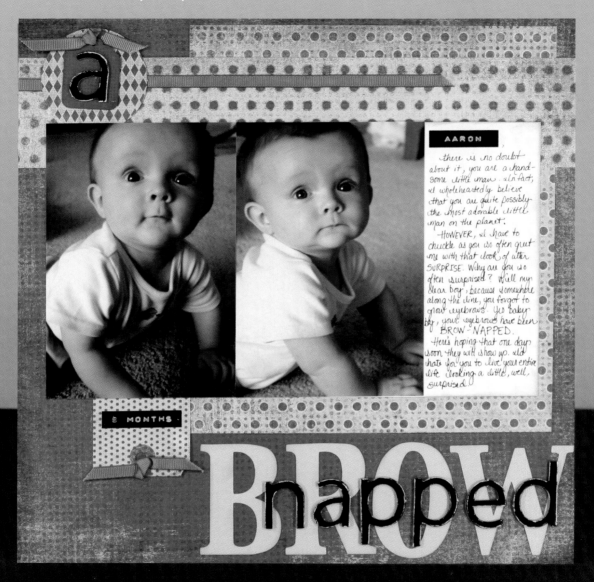

AARON, there is no doubt about it, you are a handsome little man. In fact, I wholeheartedly believe that you are quite possibly the most adorable little man on the planet.

HOWEVER, I have to chuckle as you so often greet me with that look of utter SURPRISE. Why are you so often surprised? Well my dear boy, because somewhere along the line, you forgot to grow eyebrows. Yes baby boy, your eyebrows have been BROW-NAPPED.

Here's hoping that one day soon they will show up. And that's for you to live your entire life looking a little, well, surprised.

a

8 MONTHS

BROW napped

{ IT'S ALL IN THE DELIVERY. Kristy cracks me up with this layout. She uses a playful, loving tone to record how her boy Aaron has a permanent look of surprise on his face (due to a mysterious lack of eyebrows) that is so endearing.

Within the layout:
CAUGHT! Kyle was exploring nature when...

WARNING

CAMERA MAY CAUSE GLARE

...the click of my shutter gave away my presence. Boy-did I get a look!

{ PUN INTENDED. I laughed out loud when I saw Rita's title combined with her photo! I'm sure I have lots of camera "glares" ahead of me. Wordplay doesn't have to be complicated, but it adds a dynamic interaction between a layout's photo and journaling.

requesting the honor of your company

Conversation overheard in our car.

Me: Amanda, now you can come with me to get the movie tickets.

Amanda: I don't want to drive that far. (It is 10 minutes away)

Me: This way we can spend some time together.

Amanda: You need to buy me a shake then.

Me: What?!

Amanda: Well, that is what it is going to cost you if you want me to be seen with you. *said with a big grin on her teasing face. She was teasing you know. Well, mostly teasing.

Princess Amanda

long may she reign! long may she reign!

{ QUEENLY CONVERSATION. What caught my eye about this layout was the fun design, but what really drew me in was the playful relationship that is obvious between mother and daughter. What a fun thing to record!

OUCHIES by Kara Henry..........................99

Cardstock: Bazzill Basics; Patterned paper: Chatterbox; Chipboard letters: Making Memories; Ribbon: Embellish It!, Making Memories, Michaels, unknown; Metal words: KI Memories; Pen: American Crafts; Paint: Delta; Font: Chestnuts, from twopeasinabucket.com

Notice how Kara accentuated her journaling by cutting out a thin cardboard circle to frame it, then doodled dots around the edge. To make these adorable ribbon embellishments, punch a cardboard circle, layer and adhere pieces of ribbon on it in different directions until they form a complete circle; adhere a metal word in the middle and attach entire piece to layout.

SELF PORTRAIT by Kara Henry..........................100

Cardstock: Bazzill Basics; Patterned paper, die cuts: KI Memories; Stamps: Green Grass Stamps; Thread: Coats and Clark; Brads: Making Memories; Ink: ColorBox, Tsukineko

Keep your child's first self-portrait in a cute layout like this one. Place it next to a photographed picture of your child, cover the seams of paper with stitching, paint around the border of the page, and add lettering and embellishments like some hand-sewn stars.

ON MY TOES by Kara Henry..........................101

Cardstock: Bazzill Basics; Patterned paper: Provo Craft; Chipboard: Making Memories; Ink: Tsukineko; Pens: American Crafts, Sharpie

Kara made a collage of pictures and added dimension by layering chipboard letters off the top edge of the page and adhering one matted picture with a foam dot. Who says you have to keep everything confined to the page?

UNAUTHORIZED FOOD by Kara Henry..........102

Layout was created in Adobe Photoshop CS
Font: Myriad

Use a magazine ad to spark the design of a layout.

KISSY FACE by Kara Henry..........................103

Cardstock: Bazzill Basics; Patterned paper: KI Memories; Stamps: Craft supply, Making Memories; Chipboard: Heidi Swapp, Pressed Petals; Punch: Paper Shapers; Ink: Tsukineko; Pen: Zig; Acrylic paint: Delta, Making Memories

Kara uses arrows and a line of red dots to lead your eye to the title and to her journaling. You can make cute flowers like this by painting parts of your flower stamp with alternating colors.

LAUNDRY DAY by Kara Henry..........................104

Cardstock: Bazzill Basics; Paper, acrylic charm: KI Memories; Ric rac: Wrights; Flowers, brads: Making Memories; Stickers: Heidi Swapp; Button, ribbon, die cuts: Craft supply; Pen: American Crafts; Ink: Tsukineko

Don't be afraid to get creative when embellishing. Kara made flowers out of ric rac, patterned paper, brads, and an acrylic charm from KI Memories. She attached a denim flower with a cute button and made her "Day" letters from pieces of ribbon.

OH NO! MY CAMERA BROKE
by Amy Alvis..........................105

Cardstock: Bazzill Basics; Patterned paper: Chatterbox; Chipboard: KI Memories; Stickers: Doodlebug Design, SEI; Pen: Zig; Font: 2Peas Gimme Coffee, from twopeasinabucket.com

To make her flowers, Amy cut out the designs from her patterned paper. She then used a punched circle and arrow to highlight what happened to the camera.

BROW NAPPED by Kristy Lee..........................106

Cardstock: Bazzill Basics; Patterned paper, tags: Basic Grey; Chipboard: Polar Bear Press; Ribbon: Offray; Die cut: Provo Craft; Ink: ColorBox; Pen: Zig; Label maker: Dymo

To give a little more dimension to the chipboard letters, Kristy lightly distressed the edges with sandpaper. This makes the letters pop!

WARNING by Rita Shimock..........................107

Cardstock, brads: Bazzill Basics; Patterned paper: Basic Grey; Punches: QuickKutz; Rub ons: Making Memories; Ink: ColorBox; Pens: Uni-Ball Signo

Story behind the layout: "I'm sure you've all been there…the kids just want you to put the camera away. My son was in our backyard poking around with sticks and such. I was trying to be discreet and snap a few pictures, but after taking two pictures he heard my shutter and I got the biggest scowl ever."

REQUESTING THE HONOR
by Cheryl Nelson..........................108

Cardstock: Bazzill Basics; Patterned paper: SEI; Chipboard: Scenic Route Paper Co.; Flowers, sandpaper: Heidi Swapp; Paint: Apple Barrel; Pens: Uni-Ball Signo; Markers: Zig; Rhinestones: Bead Party

Cheryl used rhinestone flowers to enhance her princess theme. Notice how she doodled around her journaling.

On the Page

Many elements come together to create a great scrapbook page, each one important in it's own right. Journaling is one of the most important of those elements, yet it should fit with the flow of your page; enhancing the photo and not taking away from it. Plan your journaling to fit the design of the layout and it will be easier to read and complete the page in an aesthetically pleasing way. Here are several ideas for making your journaling not only meaningful, but an important design element as well.

Tips for working with text:
- Title (display) text should usually be size 14 point and up.
- Body text (journaling) should usually be between 8-12 points.
- Leave generous margins around all sides of body text, as this improves the look of the layout and makes it easier to read.
- Line length is important, too. Too long and it's hard for the reader to find the next line. Too short and it feels choppy to read. Line spacing can help with these problems—if you have a longer line, make a larger space between it and the next line to make it easier for the reader to find.
- Line spacing is also important when working with difficult to read fonts. Generally sans serif fonts are harder to read and need more space overall.
- Try to avoid large blocks of white (or light) text on a black background. Although this effect can be stunning, it is not a good idea when there's a lot to read, as it is hard on the eyes.
- Mixing fonts is a fun way to add whimsy and interest to a page, but be careful that they are harmonious and limit yourself to 2 or 3. Generally, fonts that are more ornate look better as titles, or when mixed with plainer fonts. Pairing sans serif and serif fonts provides a good contrast.
- Handwriting is a fantastic way to add personality to your pages. Write clearly and leave enough space so that it is easy to read. Although it takes a little more time, I like to "clean up" my handwriting a bit for my pages.
- Use classic fonts for body text and save the fun stuff for display text.

My favorite fonts

There is nothing like having a classic font you can count on to always look great! Here are a few of my favorites:

Jensen

An elegant font that is a bit small. This is one I turn to if I'm having space issues and want a classic look.

Garamond

This font has stood the test of time; it's been around for hundreds of years! A bit more interesting than Times New Roman (the most used of the serif fonts), it is a fluid, consistent font.

Goudy

Another serif font that is both graceful and a little quirky. Good for display or body text.

Futura

Probably my favorite sans serif font. This one is so versatile; it's whimsical and sturdy at the same time. Use the lighter versions for body text and bolder ones for titles. Green Grass Stamps makes a great set of lowercase Futura I love for titles.

AdvantGarde

I like this one for a more playful and overtly san serif look.

Kabel

Another quirky typeface that is also a classic. I love its round O's and the diamonds on the "i" and "j."

Every so often, you just need a little spice or cuteness! Here are some of the fonts I turn to and websites where you can download them (free!):

Problem Secretary

A very cool typewriter font that is distressed just the right amount. (dafont.com)

2peas Tubby

Great whimsical font that's appropriate for both journaling and titles. (twopeasinabucket.com)

Freebooter Script

Script-y and formal, but also has a sense of fun. (dafont.com)

Rebekah's Birthday

A fun, freestyle font if you're hesitant to doodle a title by hand. Fontwerks has a set of clear acrylic stamps in this font. (searchfreefonts.com)

Teen Light

A fun take on traditional san serif; as a bonus, it comes in different weights. (searchfreefonts.com)

Selfish

A pretty, distressed script font. (dafont.com)

Steelfish

One of my favorite fonts—a sans serif with attitude. (dafont.com)

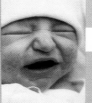
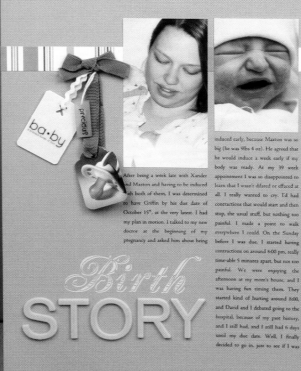

DESIGN A MAGAZINE ARTICLE. Getting large amounts of text on a page can be a challenge for us scrapbookers. This journaling is clean and easy to read; the columns of text are reminiscent of an article in a magazine. I formatted my text in Microsoft Word before printing, then cropped my photos to line up with the columns.

july 17, 2005

compilation

xander

Xander, one of the most fascinating things about being a parent is seeing yourself in your child. Daddy and I talk about who got what all the time. It always reminds me of a book by L.M. Montgomery called *Emily of New Moon*. In it, Emily goes to live with relatives she's never seen before, and they talk about from whom she got her features. She starts to get indignant at this and says, "You make me feel as if I was made up of scraps and patches!" Well, I hope we don't make you feel that way, but it's so interesting to do. You are made up of so many genes, a legacy from your ancestors, but you are uniquely your own compilation of these genes, and I think that is what makes it so interesting to see where things came from.

Now, for a breakdown of the things Daddy and I often talk about. Exhibit A is a photo of Daddy when he was about your age. Exhibit H is a photo of me around the same age. It wasn't until I started comparing this photo to yours that I really realized how much you looked like me. I usually think you look a lot like your dad. Exhibit B is a close up of your eye color and long lashes, both of

which you got from your daddy. Your eyes are almost the exact same color of hazel-y green. Exhibit C is your adorable smile. Your lips are more like Daddy's but I think you get the shape of your smile from me. The slightly crooked teeth, well, that's from both of us. Sorry about that. Exhibit D is your hair color. It always seems a bit dark in photos, but you are pretty light blond. You get that from both of us, although Daddy's hair went darker sooner than mine did. I bet you'll end up with fairly dark hair. Exhibit E is your hairline. This is all Daddy. Exhibit F is your eyebrows and your little creases under the eye. The bushiness is from daddy, but the shape of your eyebrows is mine. And you got my little under-eye creases, which were inherited from my Grandma Pond. Exhibit G is your face shape. I think you have your Daddy's wide-set eyes and wide forehead. You may have his chin as well, but it's a little young to tell exactly. And lastly, Exhibit X, my Xander-man, a sweet, little being with a huge soul that I had the privilege of helping to create (along with Daddy and your Heavenly Father). Pumpkin, I love every last one of your "scraps and patches."

THINK: CATALOG. This is another layout with a large amount of text, and I knew I'd need two pages to fit it all in. I'm comparing my son's features to both my husband and myself, so I thought it would be fun to letter the photos and then refer to them in the journaling. If you have a large block of text, try sketching the layout first to make sure you leave yourself enough room for it all. I like to do a rough sketch, print my journaling and then work it into my final design.

This summer, I've been taking the boys out in the front yard to play almost every day. I love to sit in the sunshine while they play. They run around, play with squirt guns or ride trikes. It's not so easy to convince them to go inside after we're done. To soften the blow I promise (ok, bribe them with) Otter Pops. Even Griffin gets his own.

popsicle

bribe

summer 2006

{ SHAPE IT UP. This is an example of one of my favorite layout "formulas." I group the photo, title and journaling in a column and then tie it together with other elements. Treat your text like any other element on the page and integrate it into your design. Notice how if you draw imaginary squares around each of the major elements on this layout, the shape is interesting and balanced.

So beautiful.
So peaceful.
So in love
So joyful.
So perfect.

APR 0 8 2006

brett & april

KEEP IT LIGHT. I needed the journaling to fit in a small spot on this page and not distract from the beautiful photographs of my brother-in-law's wedding. I choose to do short journaling strips instead of a block of text so that it would be readable, but not heavy enough to take away from the design of the layout.

Where did you get such eyes, little boy? Eyes like yours make me believe that your soul was alive, developed, aware, before it ever came to be in your tiny body. To me, they tell of your hopes for this life, of the grief that may come, of your potential waiting to be fulfilled—the possibility of the future. How can you be so young and so full of these things?

an old soul

NOV 17 2006

{ PLAY TAG. On this layout, I used a tag to hold my printed text. More interesting than just a plain block of text would have been, it definitely added to the design and feel of the page. I also paired a classic serif font for the journaling with an elegant script font for the title; together they match the serious and reflective mood of the layout.

Journaling on layout: I came in this morning to find you both "reading" Xander's scriptures on the couch. Daddy & I have started doing our personal scripture study in the mornings and you noticed it. It made me pause and think that the example we set for our children has a powerful influence. I need to be more careful about what I do & say.

the
POWER
of
example

JUL 1 1 2006

JUGGLE. When I made this layout, I knew the subject of the page, the content of the journaling, and even where it would go. However, I didn't actually compose my writing until I was otherwise finished with the page because I wasn't sure exactly how much room I would have. If you are having a hard time getting the journaling to fit in the space you have, consider which details are really important and pare down the rest. It's a tricky balance between space, design constraints and what you want to include—sometimes you just have to compromise a little in each area. Make it work!

Oh yes, our third child is a picky eater. I'm talking he likes his rice cereal plain and breastmilk. That's it. You try to give him something else, he goes through a whole range of facial expressions, contortions and gagging. I know he can't really help it, but boy, does he have a flair for the dramatic. I guess he resembles me in more than just looks! These are from the first time I gave him rice cereal. I had the gall to mix it with formula. Hopefully it will get better, and this is just the initial reaction. Poor little guy.

1st food FACES

The I'm-worried-and-I'm-covered-in-cereal-which-is-really-not-that-comfortable face

The I'm-not-happy-about-this-situtaion-and-if-you-don't-stop-I-will-cry-Also-I-am-disgusted face

The What-are-you-doing-Are-you-crazy-I-don't-trust-you face

The Please-help-me-Mom-I-need-help-I-can't-believe-you-are-feeding-this-to-me-help face

{ MAKE COLORFUL CAPTIONS. This page has captions for each photo, with an introduction in the block of text at the top. I wanted the captions to stand on their own, however, so I made them as interesting as possible. This set-up can work for all kinds of pages where the photos need to be individually explained. For a fun look, I printed mine on paper torn from a notebook and clipped them in place.

I'm so delighted with how well Griffin is already fitting into our family. With Xander, it was love at first sight. Even though he is barely three, he loves to help. He will tell me when Griffin is crying or ask me what is wrong with him—he even tries to give him his binki. The other day at the doctor's office, Xander couldn't see Griffin's face, and he told Daddy that he wanted to check on Griffin, to see if he was happy. Once he saw his face, he said, "Yep, he's happy." This interest sometimes has some unexpected side effects, like the other day I could see Xander was giving Griffin a Chex to eat. Luckily, he was just sticking his tongue in and out, the piece of cereal stuck to it, and I fished it out quickly. This is why Griffin is practically glued to my side!

Some days are a challenge, but I love that my boys are so close in age. Xander and Maxton are already inseparable. A few weeks ago, Maxton woke up from his nap and Xander was at Grandma's house. He ran around the house, looking, saying, "Where's Nan-noo?" If I give Max a piece of candy, he asks for one to share with Xander. I know these three will have so much fun growing up together, trying out piano lessons and different sports together—they will even all be in high school at the same time. I we'll get there all too quickly, so I'm enjoying today with all its challenges and joys. I love moments like the one in this photo, where Xander bends over his new little brother, gives him a kiss and says, "Hi, Baby Griffin. He's a little baby. He's so-o-o-o-o cute. He's so-o-o-o big. I love you, Baby Griffin."

brothers: inseparable

december 2005

{ BE COMPUTER-SAVVY. Another way to fit large amounts of text on a background is to wrap it around the photos. To make sure I had the right amount of space left for the photos, I used Microsoft Word to type my journaling, then drew a box the size of my photos on the page. I used the text wrapping tool to format the paragraphs, then changed the black line to no line. If you use this method, leave equal margins around the photos for a clean, professional look.

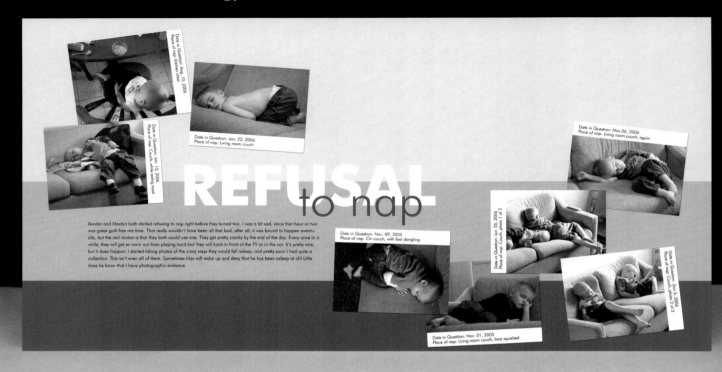

Date in Question: Aug. 10, 2006
Place of nap: Kitchen chair

Date in Question: Jan. 22, 2006
Place of nap: Living room couch

Date in Question: Jan. 10, 2006
Place of nap: Couch, while eating toast

Date in Question: May 06, 2006
Place of nap: Living room couch, again

REFUSAL to nap

Date in Question: Jun. 05, 2006
Place of nap: Couch, photo 1 of 2

Date in Question: Jun. 5, 2006
Place of nap: Couch, photo 2 of 2

Date in Question: Nov. 09, 2005
Place of nap: On couch, with foot dangling

Date in Question: Nov. 01, 2005
Place of nap: Living room couch, face squished

Xander and Maxton both started refusing to nap right before they turned two. I was a bit sad, since that hour or two was great guilt-free me time. That really wouldn't have been all that bad, after all, it was bound to happen eventually, but the real stinker is that they both could use one. They get pretty cranky by the end of the day. Every once in a while, they will get so worn out from playing hard that they will konk in front of the TV or in the car. It's pretty rare, but it does happen. I started taking photos of the crazy ways they would fall asleep, and pretty soon I had quite a collection. This isn't even all of them. Sometimes Max will wake up and deny that he has been asleep at all! Little does he know that I have photographic evidence.

{ CONSIDER READABILITY. The line length on the body of this layout is quite long. To make it easier to read, I allowed a lot of space between the lines and left out any distracting background elements.

Griffin, lately, you've been Mr. Sunshine. When I showed these photos to Daddy, he said the one of you standing by the couch reminds him of the way you stand right there, wave and say, "Bye, Dad," when he leaves for work. If Aunt Melissa or Grandma stop by, as soon as you hear a new voice, you are racing on hands and knees to the door to get a hello hug. Yep, you are pretty cute + totally loveable!

LITTLE sunShiNe

BREAK UP YOUR JOURNALING BOX. This layout also uses text wrapped around a photo; however, I handwrote my journaling. I usually draw lines with a Chatterbox Journaling Genie, then write lightly in pencil, then go over it again with a scrapbook pen. Notice how I left a margin around the photo and towards the edge of the layout. Doing so makes the text feel like it has room to breathe and also improves readability. Writing in pencil first helps me make sure everything will fit.

JUN 27 2006

You three are growing up so fast. I'm sorry if I get a little crazy with the camera; it's just I don't want to miss a thing. I love recording your milestones, your funny quirks, the events and moments that make up our family life. It's because of you that I love scrapbooking. Because I don't want to forget ANYTHING.

because of *you*

WRITE ABOUT WHY YOU DO IT. I just love this photo of me and my three boys, and decided to journal about why I scrapbook in the first place—so I can remember all the memories we make as a family. I drew lines on white cardstock to write on, then tucked part of it under the photo.

Cardstock: Bazzill Basics; Paper: Chatterbox; Sticker, tag: Pebbles, Inc.; Acrylic charm: Doodlebug Design; Rub ons, plastic letters: Heidi Swapp; Ric rac: Wrights; Ribbon: Embellish It!; Font: Jensen

Divide your journaling into three columns before printing, leaving room at the top for cropped photos

Cardstock: Bazzill Basics, Making Memories; Patterned paper: MOD; Stamps: Green Grass Stamps; Rub ons: Scrapworks; Floss: DMC; Thread: Coats and Clark; Letter tile: Deluxe Designs; Stickers: Doodlebug Design; Ink: Tsukineko; Paint: Delta; Font: Times New Roman

Kara made her layout out of close-ups of her to son to compare where he got his specific features from, her husband or her. To add interest to her title she stitched around some of the edges.

Cardstock: Craft supply; Patterned paper: American Crafts; Stamps: L'il Davis Designs; Chipboard: Basic Grey; Hole reinforcers: Office supply; Pen: Zig; Paint: Delta, Making Memories

Kara paired hole reinforcers with strips of patterned paper as a creative and unique way to break up her page.

Cardstock: Bazzill Basics; Patterned paper: My Mind's Eye; Rub ons: American Crafts, Heidi Swapp; Stamp: Office supply; Pen: Zig; Ink: Making Memories, Tsukineko

Kara made this layout clean and simple to put the focus on her pictures. She matted the photos on white cardstock and used the same cardstock for her journaling. She added rub on letters and a flourish in the corner of her large photo.

Paper: My Mind's Eye; Lace: Paperposies.com; Frames: Making Memories; Rub ons: American Crafts, Heidi Swapp; Flower, brad: Craft supply; Date stamp: Office supply; Ink: Memories, Tsukineko; Font: Goudy OlSt BT

Kara cut the cream colored frame in half and used it like a photo corner. She also created a photo corner out of a stretch of lace to add an antiqued look to her layout to tie in with her theme.

Cardstock, flowers: Bazzill Basics; Paper: Scrapworks; Stickers: American Crafts; Brads: All My Memories; Rub ons: K & Company; Stamps: Office supply; Pen: Zig

Add interest to your pages by attaching flowers with big silver brads like those Kara used from All My Memories.

Cardstock: Bazzill Basics; Paper: Chatterbox; Rub ons, clips, acrylic paint: Making Memories; Stickers: Mrs. Grossman's; Stamps: Heidi Swapp; Font: Arial

Document your baby's first food faces by placing photos of their different expressions side-by-side and using fun clips above to hold descriptions of what they may be thinking in each picture.

Cardstock: Bazzill Basics, Paperbilities; Stamps, brads: Making Memories; Stickers: American Crafts; Acrylic paint: Delta; Trim and mat board: Craft supply; Pen: Zig; Ink: Tsukineko; Font: Futura Lt BT

Using a black and white color scheme lends itself to a lot of possibilities. Kara reversed the colors of the letters, stamps, and even the photo corner at the edge of the page to make them really stand out.

Layout was created in Adobe Photoshop CS
Font: Futura

Cardstock: Bazzill Basics; Paper: Chatterbox, College Press; Rub ons: Doodlebug Design, Heidi Swapp; Photo corners: Heidi Swapp; Date stamp: Office supply; Label maker: Dymo; Pen: Signo; Ink: Tsukineko; Paint: Making Memories

To copy this background, layer strips of patterned paper horizontally and vertically as shown then paint dots along the top and right edges. You're then ready to add your pictures, rub ons, accents, and journaling.

Cardstock: Bazzill Basics; Patterned paper: Fontwerks, KI Memories, Gin-X; Chipboard: Flair Designs; Stamps: Green Grass Stamps; Date stamp: Office supply; Pen: Zig; Ink: Tsukineko, Memories

Guest Journaling

DELEGATION. MAYBE IT'S BECAUSE I'm an oldest child, but I like being in charge. However, on pages where I'm having a difficult time thinking up the journaling, it's a relief to pass it on to someone else, especially if they were more involved in the story than I was. I've found my family members are pretty good about helping with the journaling; it gives them a chance to have a voice in my scrapbooks and a different perspective is a welcome change. So don't hesitate to get some journaling help on your next layouts—you might find that they become some of your most favorite!

Who you may want to include as guest journalers:
- Parents and grandparents
- Your siblings and friends
- Your children and their friends
- A close friend of the family
- Your child's favorite teacher
- A co-worker
- A religious leader

Remember, you can keep it informal by asking them just a few questions and jotting down their answers later.

Turn to the end of this section for a list of supplies.

One of the things that Kara and I have learned over five years of marriage is to compromise. I think we've become very good at picking our battles, and giving and taking a little when we need to. Kara is more likely to suggest ideas concerning the kids, and also more likely not to give in when it comes to how to raise them. In general though, I think I'm a little more stubborn than her, and if I choose to defend a stance, I'm hard to budge from it. We're both pretty good at compromising though. I usually come up with an idea for a compromise when we are deadlocked about something, but Kara always recognizes it and meets me in the middle. I'm more likely to give in on physical things that Kara wants, clothes, scrapbooking stuff, etc...but she is more likely to give in to my ideas and reasoning, since I argue things very logically.

it's not all rainbows and butterflies,

it's compromise that moves us along

Our dynamics are very good, and we talk about everything before it gets to a boiling point, so we hardly ever fight, and never yell at each other. I am truly grateful to have a wife who listens to me, and shares her feelings with me too. It truly is compromise that keeps our relationship healthy.

OCT 08 2006

{ MODERN COMMUNICATION COUNTS. The journaling for this came from a conversation my husband and I had over instant messenger. I didn't realize that he felt this way, but I really enjoyed hearing his perspective. I asked him to write up the things he'd said to go along with this photo, a favorite that he has hanging in his office at work. Be on the lookout for other people's perspectives; they can spark a great scrapbook page!

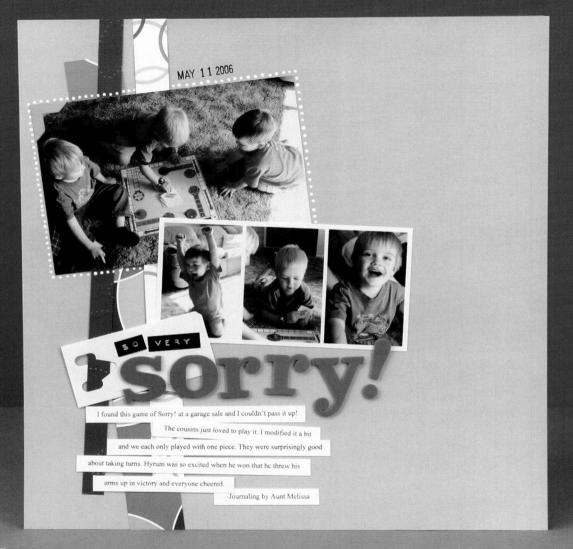

MAY 11 2006

SO VERY **Sorry!**

I found this game of Sorry! at a garage sale and I couldn't pass it up!

The cousins just loved to play it. I modified it a bit

and we each only played with one piece. They were surprisingly good

about taking turns. Hyrum was so excited when he won that he threw his

arms up in victory and everyone cheered.

—Journaling by Aunt Melissa

BEG, BORROW, STEAL. My sister did her layout of this game of Sorry! before I had a chance to finish mine. It was so cute and the journaling so perfect that I asked if I could borrow her journaling for my own page! If you have someone close to you who scrapbooks, this is a great way to get some journaling on topics that you've both scrapped. With permission, you could also use the blogs of people you regularly get together with.

Griffin was such a sweet little baby. He would

always reach up and touch your face. You

would expect him to grab a fist full of cheek

or lip any second like most kids do, but he

would just rub his hand so gently over your

face. He is definitely a more mild-mannered

boy than we're used to around here.

– Journaling by Daddy

LOVE
CHEEKS
DADDY

so soft

MAR 2 6 2006

GIVE CREDIT. After I asked David to write the journaling for this layout, I realized that you couldn't tell who exactly had written it, so I added the attribution to make it clearer. Along those lines, I realized that if my albums ever got broken up (I just use three ring binders to keep the pages together), it could get confusing as to who made the page. As a result, I've started getting in the habit of writing my full name on the back, along with the date the page was made, and the names of anyone in the photographs.

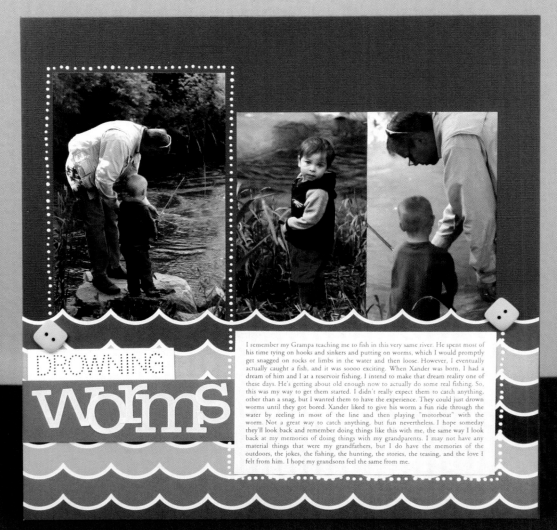

I remember my Grampa teaching me to fish in this very same river. He spent most of his time tying on hooks and sinkers and putting on worms, which I would promptly get snagged on rocks or limbs in the water and then loose. However, I eventually actually caught a fish, and it was soooo exciting. When Xander was born, I had a dream of him and I at a reservoir fishing. I intend to make that dream reality one of these days. He's getting about old enough now to actually do some real fishing. So, this was my way to get them started. I didn't really expect them to catch anything, other than a snag, but I wanted them to have the experience. They could just drown worms until they got bored. Xander liked to give his worm a fun ride through the water by reeling in most of the line and then playing "motorboat" with the worm. Not a great way to catch anything, but fun nevertheless. I hope someday they'll look back and remember doing things like this with me, the same way I look back at my memories of doing things with my grandparents. I may not have any material things that were my grandfathers, but I do have the memories of the outdoors, the jokes, the fishing, the hunting, the stories, the teasing, and the love I felt from him. I hope my grandsons feel the same from me.

{ NO PRESSURE. Sometimes it's hard to get a family member pinned down to do any journaling. In spite of their best intentions, they may be intimidated, stumped about what to write or they may simply forget. I wanted my dad's perspective on these photos, so I emailed him and asked him to write his thoughts in a reply. This is a great, no pressure approach that makes it easy for your "guest journaler" to answer you in their own time and not feel rushed. (If you have specific pictures in mind, attach them to the email.) When I read the journaling my dad wrote, I laughed and may have even teared up a bit at the end. My father is such a wonderful grandparent—my children are so lucky.

my

is someone who...

I LOVE my

GrandPa

We go to visit in CALIFORNIA | Gives me POKER CHIPS | instead of potato chips

Puts a tomato in my eggs to add a little RED | WOW! | is turning 87 years old today!

WALKS | 2 miles every day | May be WRINKLED | but is still full of life

Is so FUNNY | Is the hero of my MOM | says D@MN IT! | when he bumps his head

tells stories of when he was a champion BOXER | Is super, super | SWEET

Still lifts WEIGHTS | Is kind, wonderful and FRIENDLY

{ PHRASE-A-LICIOUS. What caught my attention on this layout was the bold colors mixed with the journaling "blurbs." Cheryl made this layout on her grandfather's 87th birthday and it's easy to tell how much she admires him from the details she chose to include in her journaling. Finish off Cheryl's title phrase when making a layout about someone special to you, or enlist the help of family members to include their thoughts, too.

{ INCLUDE A CHILD'S NOTE. Shaunte captured her son's fun personality by showing both a goofy photo and the note he wrote. She didn't need much journaling beyond the title; it perfectly sets up the rest of the layout.

I wasn't there the day Emma got her first big kid bicycle, but I can imagine what it must have been like. Out of the rows and rows of pink and purple princess bicycles, with baskets and handlebar streamers, the red "Mountain Cub" beckoned to her.

Like most first big kid bicycles, the Mountain Cub came with training wheels. They got it home, and my mom attached an old jump rope to the front so she should tug a determined, but still small, Emma around the neighborhood.

Emma grew, the jump rope came off, a very fashionable bell was added, but the training wheels stayed... until one day recently when the wrench came out and Emma got brave.

She convinced me at first to take off just one wheel, but it only took a few (very slanted) trips up and down the street for me to realize this wasn't the best plan. Emma put up a bit of a fight, but the other wheel came off too. It was time to get serious.

"Don't let go!" And I didn't. Emma peddled and I ran beside her, one hand on the handlebars and the other on the back of her seat. "Don't let go!" Up and down and back and forth we went. I was beginning to wonder how we were going to pass this point. I didn't want her to fall, and have it be my fault. I also didn't want to run behind her bike for the rest of her life.

But she did it. She surprised us both. Out of the blue, in a small-ish voice, "ok, let go now." So brave! More brave than I am, I think. "You're doing it," I said, small at first, not wanting to scare her off balance. "You're doing it! YOU'RE DOING IT! WOO HOO!" She might as well have been flying.

Now when we are in the park and pass kids Emma's age riding their bikes she whispers to me, "they still have their training wheels."

YOU DID IT

WHAT training WHEELS?

{ OUT OF THE MOUTHS OF BABES... Mara's daughter is still a bit young to write her own journaling, so she included lots of verbatim quotes to tell the story of how she learned to ride a bike without training wheels. Including lots of details from her daughter's perspective makes the story interesting.

{ TAKE TURNS. I thought I was the only one cruel enough to make my husband write journaling for my layouts, but Dana did it, too—all right! Her layout showcases a "he said, she said" perspective on what marriage is all about. What a fun idea!

He said – "Marriage is the most loving, trying, painful, comforting union. This union can create offspring that can teach you a new kind of life and love. A life that some refuse, but those who do accept it, the reward is indescribable. Marriage is not a constant feeling of happiness, but a lifelong bout of hard work that is worth every drop of sweat till the Lord calls us home. Marriage with you is my personal rollercoaster, ups and downs, and my favorite the looping loops. When we fight is causes me horrific pain in my heart but I know that we will come through stronger in the end. The love that I share for you is like no other. It is one that is forgiving, forgetful, compassionate, romantic (at heart), loving, caring, and most of all emotional. Marriage is about creating and completing the other half of yourself, and you do that for me. I love you."

She said – "I think it is easy to fall in love with the idea of marriage and lose sight of how much work it actually requires. No one tells you that love alone can not and will not carry you through the rough spots. You have to be very devoted to your partner. If you are, marriage is full of blessings."

Cardstock, flower: Bazzill Basics; Paper: MOD; Stickers: Doodlebug Design, KI Memories, MOD; Brad: Craft supply; Pen: Zig; Stamp, hole reinforcement stickers: Office supply; Ink: ColorBox; Font: AvantGarde

To highlight a specific word in your title, attach it to a brightly colored strip of cardstock that extends the width of the page, then adhere a flower on the end with a rhinestone brad. Notice how Kara incorporated the colors of her patterned paper into everything else on the page.

Cardstock, paper, stickers: American Crafts; Tag: Pebbles, Inc.; Label maker: Dymo; Photo corner: Heidi Swapp; Date stamp; Office supply; Ink: Tsukineko; Paint: Delta; Font: Times New Roman

Try different ways to frame your pictures for varying effects. Kara printed out a row pictures with a thin white frame around each, filmstrip style, then framed her other picture with a photo corner and painted dots around the edge for a more personal touch.

Cardstock: Bazzill Basics; Patterned paper, chipboard: Basic Grey; Rub ons: American Crafts; Stickers: Pebbles, Inc.; Thread: Coats and Clark; Date stamp: Office supply; Flowers: Heidi Swapp; Ink: ColorBox; Font: Garamond

Kara added a lot of texture to this page with the zigzag stitching around the picture and the flower to coordinate with the strong texture in her photo.

Cardstock: Bazzill Basics; Patterned paper, buttons, rub ons, stickers: American Crafts; Paint: Delta; Font: Garamond

Kara used this bold patterned paper from American Crafts to give the illusion of waves.

Cardstock: Bazzill Basics; Patterned paper: Scenic Route Paper Co.; Ribbon: May Arts; Chipboard, acrylic heart: Heidi Swapp; Buttons, paper clips: Craft supply; Rub ons: Doodlebug Design; Stickers: American Crafts; Ink: StazOn; Pens: Uni-Ball Signo; Markers: Zig; Font: 2 Peas High Tide, from Autumn Leaves; Other: Cotton thread

Cardstock: Prism; Patterned paper: Basic Grey, Top Line Creations; Mailbox letter: Making Memories; Stickers: American Crafts; Tab: Avery; Label maker: Dymo; Photo corners: Canson

Shaunte used her son Jayden's letter to the tooth fairy as her journaling for this page, providing an accurate depiction of how a 9 year old tries to negotiate for what he wants.

Cardstock: Bazzill Basics; Patterned paper, chipboard: Scenic Route Paper Co.; Brads: Cactus Pink; Ribbon: American Crafts, L'il Davis Designs; Hole punch: Walgreens; Circle cutter: Creative Memories, Label maker: Dymo; Corner rounder: EK Success; Stamps: Leave Memories; Ink: StazOn; Font: Batang; Photography: Eileen Finucane

Mara used circles on her page to represent the wheels of the bicycle. She punched circles from patterned paper and punched out the middle to create rings. To accentuate the wheel in the picture, she punched small yellow circles and adhered them around the wheel.

Cardstock: Bazzill Basics; Patterned paper, rub ons: Basic Grey; Eyelets: American Crafts; Brads: Queen & Co.; Ribbon: Offray; Chipboard, decorative tape: Heidi Swapp; Tape: Dynamo; Stamps: Autumn Leaves; Ink: StazOn; Paint: Palid; Die cutter: Wishblade; Pens: EK Success, Zig; Font: Arial

Dana created a panel to record her and her husband's thoughts on marriage. Their responses are tucked underneath their pictures with a pull tab. She laced up their respective sides with brads and ribbon to represent being joined together.

Guest Journaling

Special Occasions

WHETHER IT'S A WEDDING OR HALLOWEEN, the birth of a new baby or Father's Day, everyone has pictures of milestone events—occasions you want to record in a special way. I often find myself trying to make the layouts about these events just perfect, which usually only manages to slow me down and prevent me from getting them done. Other times I feel like I'm writing more or less the same thing from year to year. This section is designed to get you thinking about how to add a little spice to these layouts. I find that if you just relax and focus on your journaling, you'll be well on your way to creating pages that will beautifully record the memories of your special occasions.

More ways to approach special occasions:

- Don't feel like you have to scrapbook every photo. Sometimes one photo can say what you want and sometimes you need more. I put the photos that I don't scrapbook into a regular photo album with no guilt!
- Get perspectives from different family members and include them on a page.
- Even if you don't scrapbook the pictures for a while, do jot down a little journaling. If you're like me and forget to do this every time, check emails or blogs for more details and ask family members what they remember.
- Combine photos from an activity that spans different years on one page and journal about the tradition. (For example, making gingerbread houses every year at Christmastime.)

Turn to the end of this section for a list of supplies.

This year, we decided you were probably old enough to enjoy a birthday party with a few friends. We went all out and got a piñata, helium-filled balloons, streamers, and a huge cake from Costco, all with a super hero theme in mind. Except for the chocolate cake. We got that because Daddy + I love it and you didn't care. I sewed a cape for each guest as party favors, but I left it for the last minute + I was frantically sewing when Daddy got home.

Your cousin Tate, our next-door neighbor Hyrum, your cousin Hyrum + Max were the main guests w/ a few little sisters + Griff

as welcome tag-alongs. You were so excited about everything. You were particularly eager to blow out your candles. Daddy let them, we both turned to finish gathering stragglers from the living room, + I turned back just in time to see you blow out your candles, before we even had a chance to sing to you. DO OVER! Four is old enough to tear through wrapping paper w/out any help. You got tons of presents. Then we set up the race track Grandparents Stephens got you + that was how we ended the party. Yep, it was for sure a

super party

{ INCLUDE UNIQUE DETAILS. Birthday parties are notoriously hard to journal. So my approach for this layout was to share as many of the little details as I could. I probably wouldn't forget that it was a superhero theme or that we had a piñata, but I could easily forget that Xander blew out his candles before we had a chance to sing to him and that we put off party preparations until the last minute (oops). For big events, it helps to focus on the little details that will make it different each year.

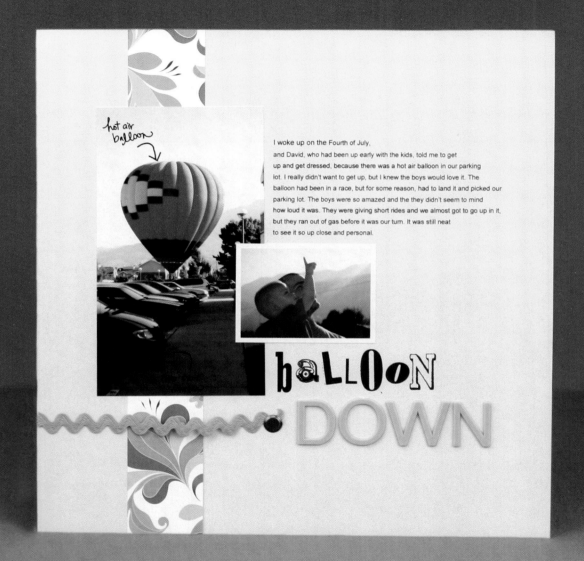

hot air balloon

I woke up on the Fourth of July, and David, who had been up early with the kids, told me to get up and get dressed, because there was a hot air balloon in our parking lot. I really didn't want to get up, but I knew the boys would love it. The balloon had been in a race, but for some reason, had to land it and picked our parking lot. The boys were so amazed and the they didn't seem to mind how loud it was. They were giving short rides and we almost got to go up in it, but they ran out of gas before it was our turn. It was still neat to see it so up close and personal.

bALLOoN DOWN

{ GO BEYOND THE PARADE. I almost didn't get to see this happen; I came close to sleeping through the whole thing. I love doing event pages that focus on the little things that make a holiday special. There's no other time besides the 4th of July when a hot air balloon would chance to land in our parking lot.

136

NOT a GREAT
halloween

OCT 3 1 2005

{ DON'T SUGAR-COAT IT. When I look back at this Halloween, I honestly cannot imagine what I was thinking trying to pack so many things into one day, with a three-week-old baby to boot! The journaling was taken from my blog entry and has a bit of an exasperated tone, but that's how it really was and I want to remember it that way.

painting pumpkins

October 7, 2005

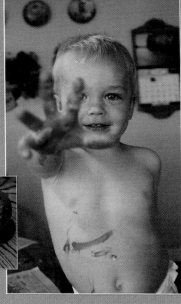

Their hands were going so fast it was hard to get clear photos of them! They were so excited and it didn't take long at all to catch on to what they were supposed to do.

The boys had so much fun getting their hands all messy with paint. Once they got all messy, they started showing me their paint covered hands.

{ EXPLORE THE EMOTIONS BEHIND THE PHOTOS. If you've ever tried to photograph an excited child in low-light conditions...well, you know it isn't easy. Because I had so many blurry pictures of this event, I wanted to convey the reason for them in my journaling—the excitement of these three boys trying a new activity.

SANTA?

Xander, I couldn't get you away from the games to sit on Santa's lap. At one point, I convinced you to get in line, but you took off when you realized you'd have to wait. Santa showed up on Christmas morning anyway. Good thing I told him what you wanted.

NO THANKS.

Dec. 2005

SO IT DIDN'T TURN OUT HOW YOU PICTURED. This layout is about one of those times when something is really more important to the parent than the child. I could not talk Xander into sitting on Santa's lap for anything, which made me sad. I don't have a single photo of him with Santa and I wanted one! I could have talked about all the other fun he had at the Christmas party, but chose instead to focus on the more unique story of him not wanting to visit Santa.

Egg

SNATCHER

Oh my- what a sneaky baby. We lined the kids up on the fence for our annual Easter egg hunt group photo. I was snapping away when I saw Madolin casually lean over and take one of Maxton's eggs!

APR 15 2006

{ SNAP AWAY! This was one of those moments when you're taking photos and you think, "Boy, I hope I caught *that*!" I was delighted to find this picture of my niece snatching an egg among the other Easter shots I took that day. I cropped it down to highlight the moment I wanted to capture, then explained how I came to get the lucky shot.

MAY 1 4 2006

Xavier, I adore this photo of you. It was taken on Mother's Day. You fell asleep after playing hard at Grandma's house. I don't often get to see you sleeping, it was a treat to see you so peaceful, your mop of messy hair & your hand curled up by your cheek. It's the little moments like these when I am overwhelmed by how much I love you— the perfect end to my day.

a CALM UNBROKEN SLEEP

{ LOOK FOR THE UNEXPECTED. After a long day (Mother's Day, actually), my oldest son decided to take a nap. When I snapped this photo, I couldn't help but truly realize how blessed I am to be a mother. More than anything else that happened that day, this moment is preserved in my mind as a meaningful one.

SEP 2 8 2006

WHeRe'S

XaNDeR?

This photo makes me laugh. During Xander's 4th birthday party, we took all the kids outside & after a lot of coaching & a bit of help, they managed to get the piñata open. With all the excitement, cl forgot to take pictures. "Oh well," cl thought, "cl'll just get a group shot." We herded them together, cl start taking photos, then realize Xander isn't there. He'd run inside to start eating his goodies!

{ WHAT'S NOT IN THE SHOT? I got so caught up in the activities of my son's birthday party that I forgot to take pictures. Thinking I could make do with a group shot, I was snapping away before I realized the birthday boy wasn't even there! What (or who) is *not* in your pictures might be a telling detail; in this case, Xander had already skipped out to go eat candy, a funny detail that I might have otherwise missed.

Cardstock: Bazzill Basics; Paper: KI Memories; Stickers, rub ons, pen: American Crafts; Decorative scissors: Provo Craft

Crop your photos carefully so they fit in a perfect 13 x 7" block. Leave ⅛" between each for an eye-catching border.

Cardstock: Bazzill Basics; Paper: cherryArte; Plastic letters: Heidi Swapp; Brad: All My Memories; Rub ons: Making Memories; Font: Unknown

Don't be afraid to write directly on your picture, as Kara did to point out just how close the hot air balloon came to their own car.

Cardstock: Bazzill Basics; Paper: Die Cuts with a View; Brads: Craft supply; Stickers: Mrs. Grossman's; Pens: American Crafts, Sharpie; Paint: Making Memories; Foam stamps: Li'l Davis Designs; Stickers, bookplates: KI Memories; Date stamp: Office supply; Ink: Tsukineko

A little white pen can make a big impact when doodling dots on a stamped title.

Layout was created in Adobe Photoshop CS
Font: Futura

Cardstock: Bazzill Basics, KI Memories; Patterned paper, acrylic charm: KI Memories; Chipboard: Heidi Swapp; Thread: Coats and Clark; Pen: Zig; Ink: ColorBox; Acrylic paint: Making Memories

Using inked strips of cardstock staggered, layered, then stitched in place is an attention-grabbing way to do your journaling. Stitching is also a great way to lead your eye from one place to another.

Cardstock: Bazzill Basics; Paper, chipboard: Basic Grey; Stickers, acrylic letters: Heidi Swapp; Chalk: Craf-T; Rub ons: Making Memories; Date stamp: Office supply; Pen: Zig; Thread: Coats and Clark; Ink: Tsukineko

To draw attention to a specific part of your photograph, cut it out, adhere it to a piece of chipboard cut to the same size then attach it back on your layout in the same place. Using this technique, Kara draws your eyes right to the special moment.

Patterned paper: KI Memories, Office supply; Ink: ColorBox; Tags: Paperbilities; Chipboard: Heidi Swapp; Acrylic paint: Making Memories; Pen: Bic; Stamp: Office supply; Ric rac: Wrights; Appliqué: Craft supply

Appliqué patches make great accents, like the dragonfly in this layout. Look for a variety of styles and designs that will fit your layouts in craft or sewing stores.

Cardstock: Bazzill Basics; Stickers: American Crafts, Making Memories; Stamp: Office supply; Ink: Tsukineko; Pen: Signo

Kara digitally transposed her son's silhouette into the picture to remember the story about how he wasn't there.

Vacation

YOUR VACATION HAS COME and gone and you're home again with a ton of photos to scrapbook, eager to record all the fun times you had. Yet journaling on vacation layouts can easily fall into the same rhythm: We saw this, we went there, we walked forever, we hung out at the beach.

Those details are certainly important, but you can take it a step further; just a little effort before and during your trip will make your pages even more interesting. Keep a notebook in the car, and while you are driving (or at the end of each day) take just 60 seconds to scribble down some of the things you don't want to forget, even if it's only a phrase or two to remind you later. Those little details add life to your pages and will help you relive the memories.

Things you could write about:
- Each person's favorite activity, place to eat, etc.
- The souvenirs you purchased
- Things you forgot to pack
- Who you met
- What arrangements you made for your house/pets
- Something you'd never done before
- What activities you couldn't fit in this time around
- What was different & the same compared to your hometown

Turn to the end of this section for a list of supplies.

Things to remember
- So hungry at the beach, and so happy when David ran to get taco bell.
- Wandering around the art exhibits and appreciating the stunning work
- Sand everywhere
- Standing around talking
- Watching the parasailing on the lake
- Trying to wash off the sand with only one working faucet
- The boys throwing pebbles in the lake and wading in the waves
- Cold lake water
- Watching the older cousins try to row with Uncle Gregg

Beach Bum

king's beach

{ MAKE YOURSELF TAKE NOTES. This is one time when I was very glad I had written things down while they were fresh in my mind. In the car on the way home from our trip to Lake Tahoe, I took just a couple of minutes to jot down some notes about our vacation. When I pulled out the list a few months later, I was surprised that I had already forgotten about several of the items! You always think you'll remember, but forgetting at least some of the details is inevitable. Be strict with yourself and write things down right away.

hanging
out

One of the best parts of the family reunion was just hanging out with everyone at the house. The grandkids did two rounds of Bingo for prizes Grandma brought! We did puzzles. Brett + April got roped into playing Sorry with Xander about 20 times. There was a little nook upstairs where the cousins watched movies. We chased Griff, since he was just starting to cruise along furniture. Xander + Max played hard with their cousins. Everyone got to rest between activities and eat meals. I loved just enjoying the family we don't get to see enough of!

July 2006
best of times

{ PHOTOGRAPH DOWNTIME. When we visited Lake Tahoe for my husband's family reunion, we ended up spending a lot of time at the house rather than on the lake, just enjoying each other's company. During this relaxed time, I took a lot of photos and was glad I did, because some of the best memories happened then.

The boys waited outside the Las Vegas temple while David and I went in to see Uncle Brett sealed to April. The temple grounds were so beautiful, but these faces say it all. We were there from 11:30 to 3:00 and that's a long time for such little guys. They were pretty good, considering. I think they could feel the peace of the temple.

Griffin

Maxon

Xander

waiting at the temple

april 8, 2006

{ GET THE KIDS' REACTIONS. We took a trip to Las Vegas for my brother-in-law's wedding. I was surprised at how beautiful the LDS temple in Las Vegas was; I had never seen it in person before. While David and I went in to see his brother get married, our boys stayed outside on the grounds. They were so incredibly patient.

147

If I could have flown anywhere for my birthday, it would have been to New York City. Obviously.

However, I came out to Anaheim for work instead. Warm weather, food expo, Disneyland. I'll take it.

I got off the plane at Santa Ana and was happy to be here. Until the baggage carousel was turned off and my bag was nowhere to be found. The suitcase I had borrowed from my roommate was not there. I walked over to the baggage counter and the woman working checked the computer and my claim ticket.

Your bag is here. It has been scanned in.

No. It was not.

I made them look around a little more. No one can find my bag. They keep telling me that my bag is somewhere in the airport, but they are not sure where. I am getting frustrated. I need my glasses. I need my pajamas. I need to wear clean underwear tomorrow. Finally another woman calls over that she found it.

That is not my bag.

Are you sure? It has your name on the claim ticket.

Yes, I am sure that my small red bag has not magically transformed into a giant black suitcase. Yes, I am sure that is not my business card with the name Brian attached to it. Yes, I am sure that the idiot back at O'Hare needs to be fired for putting the wrong baggage claim sticker on my suitcase.

She goes back to the computer. She checks the screen and smiles at me, delighted that she has good news.

Brian was going to LaGuardia.

LaGuardia. Being the true NYC soulmate that I am, I recognize the name immediately.

My bag is in New York?

Even though I didn't make it to NYC for my birthday, somehow my suitcase decided to go without me. How ironic. And given my lifelong search for irony, you can imagine what a thrill that was. Thank goodness it arrived later the next day. Just in time for me to change my underwear and head to Disneyland.

no baGgage to claim

CLAIM #
LASK469780
PURKEY / KELLY

POSITION: LASB02
10/12/2006 15:46

{ SOMEDAY WE'LL LAUGH ABOUT THIS. When something goes awry during your vacation, as it inevitably will, make a page about the mishap so you can look back and laugh (or wince), as Kelly did here with her comedy-of-errors layout about the airport sending her bags to the opposite end of the country.

ASPIRE by Stacy Hackett

One of the best parts of our trip to Florida was our visit to Kennedy Space Center. Not because Mom loves rockets (well, not entirely) or because KSC is so darn cool (which it is). This visit to KSC rocked because it brought Kayla so very close to one of her dreams.

For several years now, Kayla has wanted to be an astronaut. To be the first woman to walk on the moon. To be the first person to go to Mars. She knows it will take a lot of hard work and dedication. She briefly flirts with other career choices, but she always comes back to her love of space. This makes me so proud for so many different reasons (so dad, too).

What a joy it was to see her on the tour at KSC, looking at the Space Shuttle launch pad, reading about other female astronauts, soaking up all the information about previous space missions. I love that you ASPIRE to great things, Kayla. I love that you have big dreams. I know you can achieve your goals, kiddo. My 4th when you walk on Mars.

{ WRITE ABOUT DEFINING MOMENTS. I love Stacy's layout about their trip to the Kennedy Space Center in Florida and how it brought her daughter one step closer to her dream of becoming an astronaut. (First woman on the moon—go Kayla!) Talk about how your children's interests influence how they experience a family vacation.

GUATE by Doris Sander

WRITE FROM THE HEART. Doris writes about a life-altering mission trip to Guatemala that lasted for more than a year. I especially admire that she included how her perspective changed after her experiences there. Although Doris lived in Guatemala for an extended period, this kind of journaling would be wonderful to do for a shorter trip (or a volunteer experience) as well. While you're on vacation, take the time to look around and write a bit about the culture you are visiting.

Cardstock: Bazzill Basics; Paper: MOD; Brad: Craft supply; Stamps: Fontwerks, Green Grass Stamps; Acrylic charms: Creative Imaginations; Ric rac: Wrights; Ink: ColorBox; Font: Times New Roman

To create a unique border, Kara cut out along the diamond pattern in her paper and adhered it to the bottom of the picture collage. She also rounded all of the edges for added visual interest.

Cardstock: Bazzill Basics; Paper: Crate Paper; Stickers: American Crafts; Ribbon: Craft supply; Tag: Making Memories; Chipboard: Li'l Davis Designs; Pen: Zig; Ink: Tsukineko

Aligning your pictures in a grid is a great way to include all of the pictures you want on your page; mat them on a block of cardstock to add a nice finishing touch.

Cardstock: Bazzill Basics; Paper: Chatterbox; Stickers: American Crafts, Li'l Davis Designs; Pearl stickers: Making Memories; Ric rac: Wrights; Clip: Craft supply; Tag: Avery; Thread: Coats and Clark; Punch: McGill; Pen: Zig; Ink: Memories

Don't be afraid to write your journaling on a sheet of notebook paper and attach it to your layout, it's convenient and adds a personal touch.

Patterned paper: KI Memories; Ribbon, stickers: American Crafts; Chipboard: Heidi Swapp; Buttons: Autumn Leaves; Font: SP Black Friday, from scrapsupply.com

Kelly used a bookplate to frame her baggage claim ticket. Using your ticket stubs and other memorabilia is a great way to help you remember your experiences.

Cardstock: KI Memories; Patterned paper: Rob and Bob Studios; Brads: Doodlebug Design, Making Memories; Ribbon: American Crafts, Bazzill Basics, KI Memories, May Arts; Chipboard: Heidi Swapp; Flowers: Prima; Ink: Tsukineko, VersaColor; Pen: Sakura; Photo corners: Canson; Other: Staples

Stacy wrote her journaling on punched circles with inked edges and added dimension by layering them. She added interest to the edge of her page by creating a border from folded ribbon pieces attached with brads and staples.

Cardstock: Bazzill Basics; Patterned paper: Autumn Leaves; Fibers: DMC; Ribbon, staples: Making Memories; Chipboard: L'il Davis Designs, Making Memories; Paint: Folk Arte; Tags: Avery; Stamps: Heidi Swapp; Ink: Tsukineko; Pen: Zig

Doris created a two-page spread with a picture collage on one side and the journaling on the other. She stamped her title over her journaling and added extra interest by stitching circles over her pictures with embroidery floss.

scrapbook
TRENDS

Your Layouts

Your Projects

YOUR BOOK

go ahead...have a party!

Now scrapbooking is fast and easy. Create a beautiful scrapbook from cover to cover in about an hour with s•e•i's 1 Hour Album kits. The kit includes the album, sheet protectors, all cardstocks, stickers, brads, buttons and simple step-by-step instructions. Available in a variety of themes and sizes. Scrapbook-in-a-box and scrapbook-in-a-bag will fit any occasion or mood...and it makes a great gift! Find them at your local scrapbook/paper arts retail store.

1 HOUR ALBUM!
•great for beginners•
•step-by-step instructions•
•all pre-cut pieces•

Party Time!

The Scrapbooker's Guide to Party Planning

Planning a birthday party? Or a fun evening together with friends? Throwing a baby or bridal shower? We've got everything you need to get that party planned from beginning to end – invitations, decorations, games, favors, thank yous and even scrapbook pages to document all the fun. With inventive ideas and a large variety of themes, this book is essential for anyone planning a party!

scrapbook TRENDS

Call 1.888.225.9199 or visit scrapbooktrendsmag.com to order today!

Pioneer Photo Albums®

Hibiscus

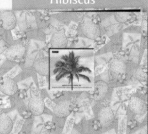
Palm Trees

Tropical Leaves

Tropical Drinks

New!

Tropical
&
Map

12" x 12" Frame Cover Top Loading

Scrapbooks

Tropical (Style No. MB-10TRP)
Map (Style No. MB-10MAP)

Globes

World Map

Travel Stickers

City Maps

Pioneer Photo Albums, Inc.
(800) 366-3686 • (818) 882-2161 • Fax: 8188826239 • pioneer@pioneerphotoalbums.com

Retail Store Directory

ONLINE STORE DIRECTORY

ALLY SCRAPS
www.allyscraps.com

BLESSINGS RECEIVED
www.stores.ebay.com/blessings-received

EXPRESSIVE SCRAPBOOKS
www.expressivescrapbooks.com

UNDERGROUND SCRAPBOOKING SUPPLY CO.
COEURD' ALENE, ID
208-664-6010
originalsbygina@hotmail.com
www.OBGunderground.com

SCRAP HAPPY KT
PO BOX 436
ELDERSBURG, MA 21784
410-549-3222

THE SCRAP STOP
www.thescrapstop.com

URBAN SCRAPPER
www.urbanscrapperonline.com

ARIZONA

BINDING MEMORIES BY IDA
1150 DUCE OF CLUBS STE C
SHOWLOW, AZ 85901
(928) 537-8116

PAPER & METAL SCRAPPERS
804 B. NORTH BEELINE HWY
SWISS VILLAGE SHOPS
PAYSON, AZ 85541
928-468-1188
paperandmetal@earthlink.net

CALIFORNIA

PAGES IN TYME
560 PINE KNOTT BLVD STE B
BIG BEAR LAKE, CA 92315
909-866-3661
M-S 10-6 SUN 10-5

SCRAPBOOK BLESSINGS
1560 NEWBURY ROAD STE 5
NEWBURY PARK, CA 91320
805-375-1568
M-Sat 9-6
service@scrapbookblessings.com
www.scrapbookblessings.com

SCRAPBOOK NOOK
444 SAN MATEO AVE.
SANBRUNO, CA 94066
650-588-3112

STAMPERS WAREHOUSE
101-G TOWN & COUNTRY DR
DANVILLE, CA 94526
(925) 362-9595

TABLE SCRAPZ
2500 E. IMPERIAL HWY SUITE 136
BREA, CA 92821
(714) 529-6887
M-F 11-7, SAT 10-6 SUN 11-5
customerservice@tablescrapz.com

COLORADO

THE TREASURE BOX
1833 E. HARMONY RD #1
FORT COLLINS, CO 80528
970-207-9939
M-F 9:30-6 TH 9:30-9
SAT 10-5

CONNECTICUT

NEW ENGLAND SCRAPBOOK CO
200 ALBANY TURNPIKE-RTE 44
CANTON, CT 06019
860-693-9197
M-tu 10-6 W-th 10-9 F-sat 10-10 Sun 12-6
www.newenglandscrapbook.com

FLORIDA

CROPPIN' CORNER
175-C NE EGLIN PKWY
FT.WALTON BEACH, FL 32548
850-581-2767
M ,W-F 9-6 TUE 9-8 SAT 9-5
www.croppincornerfl.com

RUBAN ROUGE
3454 TAMPA ROAD
PALM HARBOR, FL 34684
727-784-8600
info@rubanrougepaperarts.com
rubanrougepaperarts.com

GEORGIA

SCRAPBOOK OUTLET
PRIME OUTLET S-CALHOUN #90
CALHOUN, GA 30701
706-602-3555
I-75, EXIT 312, 40 ML N OF ATLANTA
Scrapbookoutlet.com

HAWAII

SCRAPBOOK CLUBHOUSE HAWAII
98-302 KAMEHAMEHA HWY
AIEA, HI 96701
808-486-0333
JUST 5 MINS FROM PEARL HARBOR
M 10-3, T-SAT 10-7 SUN 11-3
www.scrapbookclubhousehawaii.com

THE SCRAPPERS' DEN
719 KAMEHAMEHA HWY SUITE C201
PEARL CITY, HI 96782
808-455-4100
T-FR 10-6, SAT 10-4 SUN 11-3
www.scrappersden.com

IDAHO

CINDY'S
34 NORTH MAIN STREET
MALAD, ID 83252
208-766-2666
www.cindysscrapbooking.com

**A SCRAPPERS
& STAMPERS DELIGHT**
TIFFANY SQUARE
156 MAIN AVE N.
TWIN FALLS, ID 83301
208-736-7286
mary@scrapthatsmile.com
www.scrapthatsmile.com

CINDY'S
34 NORTH MAIN ST
MALAD, ID 83252
208-766-2666
www.cindysscrapbooking.com

ILLINOIS

MEMORIES & BEYOND
1400 C 75TH STREET
DOWNERS GROVE, IL 60516
630-271-0610
M-F 10-9, SAT 10-6, SUN 12-5
CROP NIGHT, FRI & SAT
info@memoriesbeyond.com
www.memoriesbeyond.com
www.yourscrapbookcorner.com

SCRAP N STAMP ART
901 SOUTH NEIL ST, STE B
CHAMPAIGN, IL 61820
217-352-0532
M-F 10-6, SAT 10-5, SUN 11-5
www.scrapnstampart.com

SCRAPBOOK SOURCE
557 W. NORTH AVE.
CHICAGO, IL 60610
312-440-9720
M-F 10-8, SAT 10-6, SUN 12-5
CROP NIGHT, FRIDAY
info@scrapbooksourceinc.com
www.scrapbooksourceinc.com
www.yourscrapbookcorner.com

INDIANA

SCHMITT PHOTO
4847 PLAZA EAST BLVD
EVANSVILLE, IN 47715
812-473-0245
M-F 8:30-8 SAT 9-6 SUN 1-5
www.schmittphoto.com

SCRAPAHOLICS
811 W. McGALLIARD RD.
MUNCIE, IN 47303
765-213-9900
M-F 10-6, SAT 9-4
www.scrapaholics1.com

SCRAPBOOK OUTLET
PRIME OUTLET- FREMONT #10
FREMONT, IN 46737
260-833-2767
I-69 AND 80/90 TOLL ROAD
Luv2scrapbook.com

SCRAPBOOK XANADU
520 N. STATE RD #135
GREENWOOD, IN 46142
317-885-7200
M-F 10-9 SAT 10-7 SUN 12-5
www.scrapbookxanadu.com

KENTUCKY

SCRAPBOOK OUTLET
DRY RIDGE OUTLET CENTER #1106
DY RIDGE, KY 41035
859-823-2767
I-75 25 ML S. OF CINCINNATI
Scrapbookoutlet.com

MAINE

MEMORY LANE
20 COBURN ST
AUBURN, ME 04210
207-782-1600
memorylanepages@aol.com
www.memorylanepages.com

THE MEMORYBOOK WORKSHOP
THE GRAY PLAZA
GRAY MAIN, ME 04039
207-657-4566
cindy@memorybookworkshop.com
www.memorybookworkshop.com

MY CROP PAPER SCISSOR STORE
168 FRONT STREET
FARMINGTION, ME 04938
207-778-6660
TUE-FRI 9-5:30, SAT & SUN 10-4
www.mycpsstore.com

MARYLAND

SCRAP HAPPY KT
PO BOX 436
ELDERSBURG, MD 21784
410-549-3222
www.scraphappykt.com

MASSACHUSETTS

LEAVE A LEGACY SCRAPBOOKING
1510 NEW STATE HWY RT 44 UNIT 18
RAYNHAM, MA 02767
508-880-6900
M-CLOSED, T-TH 10-8,
W,F,SAT 10-6 SUN 12-4
www.leavealegacyscrapbooking .com

MICHIGAN

PAGES IN TIME
6323 C WEST SAGINAW HWY
LANSING, MI 48917
517-327-5526

MINNESOTA

MEMORY BOX
38 N. UNION ST.
MORA, MN 55051
320-679-3439
www.memorybox.biz

MISSOURI

THE SCRAP OUTLET.COM
1320 W 40 HWY
ODESSA, MO 64076
816-230-5579
LOCATED AT THE ODESSA OUTLET MALL
www.thescrapoutlet.com
COME VISIT OUR WEB SITE FOR FREE OFFERS

NEVADA

PEBBLES IN MY POCKET
7650 W. SAHARA
LAS VEGAS, NV. 89117
702-438-9080
OPEN SEVEN DAYS A WEEK
www.pebbleslasvegas.com

NEW YORK

YOUR HAPPY PLACE
272 LARKFIELD RD
E. NORTHPORT, NY 11731
www.yourhappyplaceonline.com

NORTH CAROLINA

A PAGE IN TIME
1216-A PARKWAY DR.
GOLDSBORO, NC 27534
919-344-7884
Arlene@apgntime.com
www.apgntime.com

ENCHANTED COTTAGE
RUBBER STAMP & SCRAPBOOKS
JUST WEST OF WINSTON-SALEM
6275 SHALLOWFORD RD
LEWISVILLE, NC 27023
336-945-5889
M 10-3 T, W, F 10-5:30 TH 10-8 SAT 10-4
www.enchantedcottagenc.com

OHIO

COUNTRY CROSSING
& CROPPERS CORNER
IN FRONT OF WALMART
CORNER OF STATE RT 250
&WESTWIND DR
NORWALK,OH 44857
419-663-0496
postmaster@cropperscorner.net
www.cropperscorner.net

SCRAPBOOK OUTLET
PRIME OUTLETS- LODI #175
BURBANK, OHIO 44214
330-948-8080
I-71, EXIT 204, 20 ML S OF CLEVELAND
Scrapbookoutlet.com

OKLAHOMA

A SCRPABOOK GALLERY
12091 PERRY HWY STE 1
WEXFORD, PA 15090
724-933-9310
m-w 10-8, th 10-10, f-s 10-midnight sun 12-4
www.ascrapbookgallery.com

SCRAPBOOKS FROM THE HEART
11649 S. WESTERN AVE.
OKLAHOMA CITY, OK 73170
405-692-6491
M-S 10-6, SUN 1-5
www.scrapbooksfromtheheartokc.com

SCRAP HAPPYS
7142 S. MEMORIAL DR.
TULSA, OK 74133
918-250-0472
M-W, S 10-6 TH-F 10-8 SUN 1-5
www.scraphappys.com

OREGON

SCATTERED PICTURES
13852 NE SANDY BLVD
PORTLAND, OR 97230
503-252-1888
TU, TH,F- 10-5 W 10-8 SAT 10-4
CLOSED MON & SUN

SCRAP-A-DOODLE
354 NE NORTON SUITE 101
BEND, OR 97701
541-388-0311
scrap@scrap-a-doodle.com
www.scrap-a-doodle.com

PENNSYLVANIA

SCRAPBOOK SUPER STATION
A CRAFTERS HOME STORE
168 POINT PLAZA
BUTLER, PA 16001
724-287-4311
SUN 12-5 MON-SAT 10-9
www.scrapbookstation.com

TENNESSEE

THE CROP SHOP
7616 LEE HWY BLDG B
CHATTANOOGA, TN 37421
423-899-3515
store@cropshoponline.com
www.cropshoponline.com

TEXAS

LONE STAR
SCRAPBOOK COMPANY
27842 1-45 N.
THE WOOD LANDS, TX 77385
281-296-2296
www.lonestarscrapbook.com

NOVEL APPROACH
607 S FRIENDSWOOD DR.#15
FRIENDSWOOD, TX 77546
281-992-3137
www.booksandscraps.com

SCRAPBOOK VILLAGE
3424 FM 1092 STE 270
MISSOURI CITY, TX 77459
281-208-5251
www.thescrapbookvillage.com

VERMONT

CREATIONS ABOUND
50 N. MAIN ST SUITE 101
ST ALBANS, VT 05478
TOLL FREE 877-517-3521
info@creationsabound.com
www.creationsabound.com

VIRGINIA

ALL ABOUT SCRAPBOOK
2137 UPTON DRIVE, STE 328
VIRGINIA BEACH, VA 23454
(RED MILLS COMMONS)
757-563-9009
www.allaboutscrapbooksonline.com

WASHINGTON

A LITTLE BIT OF HEAVEN
7912 MARTIN WAY E
OLYMPIA, WA 98516
360-493-1707
OPEN 7 DAYS A WEEK,
M-SAT 10-8, SUN 11-5
www.alittlebitofheavensscrapbooking.com

SCRAPBOOKER'S DELIGHT
1160 YEA AVE
BLAINE, WA 98230
604-536-55557

WISCONSIN

THE SCRAPBOOK STORE 3
5042 S. 74TH ST.
GREENFIELD, WI 53220
262-255-2521
www.scrapbook-store.com

CANADA

**MAKING MEMORIES
WITH SCRAPBOOKING**
4415 HASTING ST
BURNABY, BC V5C 2K1
604-299-3601
makingmemories@telus.net
www.makingmemorieswithscrapbooking.com

SCRAPBOOKER'S DELIGHT
102-14936-32 AVE.
SURREY BC CANADA V4P 3R6
604-536-5557
www.scrapbookersdelight.net

SCRAPBOOK MEMORIES & MORE
#20, 975 BROADMOOR BLVD.
SHERWOOD PARK, ALBERTA CA
OPEN 7 DAYS A WEEK
HOLIDAYS 12-5
www.scrapbookmemories.ca

A SCRAPBOOKERS DREAM
15 ALLEN DR.
BOLTON, ON L7E 2B5
905-951-9544
ONLY 30 MIN. FROM DWTWN TORONTO
www.ascrapbookersdream.com

SCAPALICIOUS SCRAPBOOKS
2123 JACKLYN RD UNIT 21
VICTORIA, BC V9B 3Y1
850-474-8128
SUN 11-5 M & S 10-6 T-F 10-8
www.scrapvictoria.com

SCRAPBOOK PARADE
109, 4430 W. SAANICH RD
VICTORIA, BC V82 3E9
250-727-0372
scrappix@island.net
www.scrapbookparade.com

SCRAPBOOK CORNER
#142-1020 SHERWOOD DR.
SHERWOOK PARK, AB T8A 2G4
780-464-0284
OPEN 7 DAYS A WEEK
www.scrapbookcorner.ca

SCRAPBOOK STUDIO INC.
1890 HYDE PARK RD
LONDON, ON N6H 5L9
519-474-2665
M-F 10-9 SAT 10-5 SUN 12-5
www.scrapbookplus.com

Advertising Directory

TrendSetters

Fifteen top scrapbookers. One amazing book.

scrapbook TRENDS

GET UP CLOSE AND PERSONAL with some of the industry's hottest scrapbookers! As these women have moved to the forefront of the industry over the past few years, they have been featured in multiple publications, won a myriad of contests, created countless designs for top scrapbooking companies and also occupy positions on many design teams. But more than that, their fresh ideas, amazing creations and meaningful journaling caught our eye – they are true trendsetters as they provide inspiration to scrappers everywhere. Sneak a peek into their lives and see what inspires them as they share their favorite tips and tricks. With mini albums, cards, layouts and more, not only will they give you lots of fun ideas, but you will feel like you have several new friends. Come see why we have named these 15 ladies the Scrapbook "TrendSetters" class of 2006!